JAPANESE WAR FANTASY
1933

AN EDITED AND ANNOTATED TRANSLATION OF

"Account of the Future
US-Japan War"

BY KYOSUKE FUKUNAGA

EDITED AND
ANNOTATED BY
Jamie
Bisher

T0054608

SCHIFFER MILITARY

4880 Lower Valley Road   Atglen, PA 19310

Library of Congress Control Number: 2022944550

Designed by Jack Chappell
Cover design by Jack Chappell
Type set in Univers/Calgary/Agency/John Doe/Times

ISBN: 978-0-7643-6646-8
Printed in India

Published by Schiffer Publishing, Ltd.
4880 Lower Valley Road
Atglen, PA 19310
Phone: (610) 593-1777; Fax: (610) 593-2002
Email: Info@schifferbooks.com
Web: www.schifferbooks.com

For our complete selection of fine books on this and related subjects, please visit our website at www.schifferbooks.com. You may also write for a free catalog.

Schiffer Publishing's titles are available at special discounts for bulk purchases for sales promotions or premiums. Special editions, including personalized covers, corporate imprints, and excerpts, can be created in large quantities for special needs. For more information, contact the publisher.

We are always looking for people to write books on new and related subjects. If you have an idea for a book, please contact us at proposals@schifferbooks.com.

To Veronica, Godfrey, Natalie, and James. Even outrageous war tales pale in comparison to the frenzied excitement, drama, and tears of worry, fury,
and joy that you bring to my life.

War is not for material gains;
war is an adventure.

—Admiral Nobumasu Suetsugu,
Imperial Japanese Navy, July 1941

CONTENTS

PREFACE

During my childhood in Atlanta in the 1960s, my father, in rare moments of nostalgia, would extract a raggedy beige handkerchief box from deep in his closet. The box was magic, a genie's lamp that opened a portal to the past. . . . It held a couple of dull aluminum dog tags, three colorful service ribbons, a naval lieutenant's felt epaulet, officers' club cards from Pearl Harbor and Midway Island, and a faded snapshot of a young man—my father—wearing Navy khakis, a pith helmet, and a holstered .45 sidearm.

Opening this time capsule transformed him. His eyes fixed decades and half a world away. Then he would speak with uncharacteristic humility about his war service, even though he had abruptly abandoned a hard-won new career in journalism to join the Navy in December 1941. These precious moments with "Ole Dad" spawned my fascination with history, ultimately leading me to the dusty gray boxes of documents in the National Archives years later.

While researching World War I intelligence networks in Latin America and civil war in the Russian Far East, I was surprised to find Japanese diplomats, military and intelligence officers in both far-flung theatres working against their US counterparts. Apparently, my father's war was brewing twenty years before it erupted. US officials documented ample evidence of Japanese aggression throughout the interwar period.

Strategic risks in the Pacific transfixed American naval and military leaders even during years of depression, economic struggle, and wavering international engagement. Pearl Harbor was always an obvious strategic target, and defenses were dutifully strengthened over the years. However, timing was everything. Every year, new technology, industrial capability, and strategic moves amplified the threats. Every year, the future enemy's resolve strengthened, in no small part due to the constant drumbeat of propaganda such as Kyosuke Fukunaga's novelette. When would Japan strike? 1936? 1937? or . . . ?

The treasures of the US National Archives inspired this book. I am also grateful for the gems of knowledge that surface on the internet, and for the online resources of the Library of Congress. The Naval Historical Center (NHC) earns special gratitude for keeping their rich photographic archives easily available, while other public repositories—even the Library of Congress—seem to be limiting access and decreasing online offerings.

I owe special thanks to Kendall Aughenbaugh, the diligent archivist at the University of Maryland Library who found a rare copy of the Fukunaga book in the Gordon W. Prange Collection, and even digitized select pages for me.

I happened upon a translation of Fukunaga's war story by accident in the National Archives. I've tried to retain the original language of the military intelligence translator, even though the archaic 1930s script sounds awkward sometimes. Japanese names are stated with surnames last, as cited in US intelligence documents.

Future war between Japan and the US was a popular topic of fiction on both sides of the Pacific in the interwar years. But Fukunaga's tale was endorsed by two of the most influential admirals in the Imperial Japanese Navy (IJN). For a spell in late 1933, the complacent American public was transfixed. The Japanese American community was alarmed. Congressmen fretted. All this hoopla erupted from a box of imported pulp fiction. Alas, Fukunaga's verbose *manga* embodied Japanese admirals' fantasies of the war to come . . .

I hope that this book might answer the question: *What were they thinking?*

Jamie Bisher

Jamie Bisher asks: *What were they thinking?*

Why did Japan strike Pearl Harbor, and blatantly draw the mighty United States into war? For over eighty years this mind-boggling question has lingered. Japanese military and political leaders certainly understood that this extreme act of aggression would have dire consequences. And it did.

Japan's sneak attack on Sunday morning, December 7, 1941, crippled the American Navy's Pacific Fleet and left scores of Army Air Force planes smoldering in Hawaii. But the United States retaliated with a vengeance. Four years of relentless island to island fighting crushed Japanese forces and brought their leaders to their knees in humiliating surrender.

Now back to Bisher's thought-provoking question, why did Japan risk war against a superior power with defeat a strong possibility? Thanks to his creative sleuthing, we now see the answer that has been hiding in plain sight for over eighty years.

Published in 1933, Kyosuke Fukunaga's paperback *Nichibei-sen Miraiki* predicted in great detail a future war between Japan and the United States. The intent of Tokyo publisher Shinchosha was to assure readers, anxious about Western encroachment in the Pacific, that the powerful United States would suffer at the hands of Japan's naval fleet.

In 1933, eight years before Pearl Harbor, Fukunaga's novelette pronounced the Japanese Navy's unmistakable intent to engage America in a Pacific War, even if it had to be provoked. Admirals Kanji Kato and Nobumasa Suetsugu were among the hawks who not only devoured but promoted Fukunaga's book. They took comfort that Washington Naval Treaty restrictions would one day be terminated, but were even more confident that Japanese sailors' fighting spirit, training and ingenuity would trump American technical and numerical superiority.

American military intelligence became aware of *Nichibei-sen Miraiki*, transcribing the 119-page novelette soon after it was published. Like many of the warning signs presaging December 1941, Fukunaga's not so hidden message lay dormant. Bisher correctly points out it was the "bombshell that would reverberate from Honolulu to Washington and back to Tokyo."

Mitchell Yockelson

INTRODUCTION
The First Japanese Bombshell

HONOLULU, DECEMBER 1933

The first Japanese bombshell dropped on Hawaii in late 1933. At first glance, it appeared to be merely a crate of little comic books that were offloaded from SS *President Taft* and addressed to George Kojima's Honolulu bookstore. A second consignment would be confiscated a few days later. To US customs agents, the crates contained explosive material: a riveting techno-thriller outlining an imminent war between Japan and the United States—propaganda intended to seduce Hawaiian *nikkei* to treason. The book was written by a retired Japanese naval officer named Kyosuke Fukunaga, endorsed by admirals of the Imperial Japanese Navy (IJN), and distributed by a popular Tokyo magazine with a large domestic and international following. The provocative future war novelette was a bombshell that would reverberate from Honolulu to Washington and back to Tokyo.

The scandalous novelette was *Nichibei-sen Miraiki*, translated by American military intelligence analysts as *Account of the Future US-Japan War*. It was merely 119 pages, a pocket-sized paperback with a cover showing a US warship firing broadside as the silhouette of a distant destroyer slipped across an ominous horizon. Distributed by Tokyo publisher Shinchosha, it was one of three freebie supplements intended to entice readers to shell out 0.60 yen for the January 1934 issue of *Hinode* magazine. Shinchosha was hoping for sales, not scandal and confiscation. After all, American and European publishers had cashed in on similar future war themes.

Nichibei-sen Miraiki cover. *University of Maryland Prange collection*

War fiction and Yellow Peril fearmongering were certainly not new phenomena in 1933. A realistic 1925 novel, *The Great Pacific War*, by *London Daily Telegraph* naval correspondent Hector C. Bywater, was translated into Japanese and studied by Imperial Japanese Navy officers.[2] The dashing US war correspondent and radio commentator Floyd Gibbons capitalized on the Japanese challenge to the white supremacy myth in a 1929 serial that ran in the popular *Liberty* magazine, imagining an Asian alliance with African American freedom fighters. Resurrection of the Fu Manchu series in the early 1930s exploited Western fears of a diabolical Asian underworld. In 1934, Emperor Ming would confront Flash Gordon. Asian villains reflected US apprehension of a brewing face-off for power in the Pacific.

Japanese anxiety about US encroachment in the Pacific inspired a new genre of future war fiction. A 1913 book, *Fantasy about the Outbreak of a Japanese-American War*, described invasions of the Philippines and Hawaii, common themes in Japanese fiction. A 1914 book, *If Japan and America Fight*, added a preface by a retired admiral. General Kojiro Sato penned a detailed, thought-provoking scenario in 1921, *Japanese-America War Fantasy*. Sato's full-length novel depicted the defeat of the US fleet around Midway Island and Japan's occupation of Hawaii and invasion of California. Mexico invaded the southwestern US, and African Americans, German Americans, and Jews rebelled against the US government. A surprise attack early one Sunday morning subdued New York City and pushed a weak-willed US to beg for peace.[3] The early 1930s saw the tone and tempo of Japanese war musings grow more serious and strident, reflecting the increasing influence of militarists over Japan's politics.

In October 1932, the US naval attaché in Tokyo reported to the Office of Naval Intelligence in Washington about the explosive proliferation of Japanese pro-war publications. An outpouring of articles followed the 1930 international disarmament conference in London and the 1931 Mukden incident, which launched Japan's takeover of Manchuria. There were so many war articles on the newsstands that the naval attaché could not peruse them all. He bought a stack of newspapers and magazines and translated several that were "representative of the jingo spirit now spreading with increasing vigor throughout Japan . . . and presented a good cross section of the propaganda and war hysteria now prevailing." Conjecture about strategy and tactics predominated over puerile war fiction, and many of the writers were authorities on their subject matter.[4]

Kenzo Adachi, a retired lieutenant colonel and aviation expert, wrote, "The Alaskan Air Attack," which analyzed how long-range aircraft could bridge the gulfs between bombing targets around the northern and western Pacific.[5]

Shinsaku Hirata, a reactionary publicist known as the "Hector Bywater of Japan," churned out "The Capture of the Philippines." Hirata predicted tactical difficulties in capturing the "bases at Cavite"—Bataan and Corregidor, although the US Navy would not be much help in their defense, and concluded, "If those two [bases] were captured, then the subjugation of the whole group of islands would be much simpler than the subjugation of the Manchurian bandits."[6]

Hironori Mizuno, author of "The California Attack," was a philosopher and man of letters who could dare to lambast the militarists because he was a hero of the Russo-Japanese War. His war scenario described a successful Japanese takeover of Hawaii, carrier-launched air attacks on San Francisco, and a planned amphibious assault in Southern California. But he ventured to state that the Japanese fleet had been stretched too thin to consummate the troop landing, and that British ships had taken the upper hand in the Western Pacific while Tokyo was preoccupied with the prolonged war against the US. Mizuno was the rare pessimist among Japanese writers hammering out stories of US capitulations to the Rising Sun.[7]

Retired lieutenant commander Tota Ishimaru, a respected author of ten books on naval affairs, published "The Assault on Hawaii." It accurately forecast an alliance of the US, Great Britain, and China against Japan and prescribed that Hawaii, "the Gibraltar of the Pacific," not be invaded until the Allied fleets had been defeated in the Western Pacific. Ishimaru's fantasy included a "revolt by Japanese residents in Hawaii, . . . secretly organized and equipped," who "launched a surprise attack on the American defenders." He also credited one Maj. Elliott, a former US military attaché in Tokyo, whose own book, *The Tide of Battle*, named the best Hawaiian beaches for amphibious landings. Insecurity on both sides of the Pacific drove sales of future war tales.[8]

By December 1933, it was a different paranoia in Honolulu that prompted the confiscation of Shinchosha's explosive little novelette. "The first complaint regarding this allegedly seditious literature came from local Japanese merchants who had read copies of the story and were afraid that it would be construed as an unfriendly gesture toward America," reported the *Hawaii Hochi* newspaper on December 18 in a sincere but clumsy attempt to recap the seizure incident.[9] In fact, George Kojima, a Honolulu store owner, was at the pier to receive the *Hinode* shipment when SS *President Taft* docked.

A Japanese American clerk in the US Customs office, who knew a few Japanese characters, examined the shipment with Kojima, who fretted aloud that the novelette "was 'not so good' for distribution to the local Japanese." The clerk took home a copy and, with the help of his Japanese wife, translated it. The next morning, the clerk "informally requested" the opinion of US Army authorities at Fort Shafter. The Army informally replied "that in its opinion the [Hinode] supplement should be seized."[10] Unbeknown to the customs clerk or to the Army, Kojima had already sold 173 copies of Hinode by the time the clerk informed Kojima of the Army's opinion just one day later.

Customs officials in Honolulu promptly, perhaps rashly, ordered confiscation of the Hinode shipment, apparently on the basis of advice of the unnamed Nikkei customs clerk. They cited Section 305 of the Tariff Act of 1930 on the grounds that the novelette advocated treason against the US. George Kojima obligingly called in all the copies that he had distributed and turned them in to customs without complaint. The remainder of the seven cases of Hinode that had been delivered by the President Taft were quietly locked up. The incident went unnoticed by the public until the elegant transpacific passenger liner Chichibu Maru arrived a few days later with seventy cases more. They were consigned to three Honolulu stores, whose representatives soon arrived at customs to claim them. Customs informed them that their merchandise had been confiscated. On December 14, the Hinode seizure made news in at least four different Honolulu newspapers.[11] The wake of that publicity made waves in customs that reverberated to the agency's executive bureaucracy in Washington.

The Hinode confiscation stirred up politically sensitive controversy within the Customs Service. J. Walter Doyle, the collector of customs in Honolulu, took responsibility for the decision to confiscate. His boss in Washington, James Henry Moyle Jr., was an agile Democratic Party operator who had been the first Mormon appointed as a high federal executive in 1917. Moyle was careful to point out that the Hinode seizure was "not made on his instructions." Collector Doyle had to squelch rumors that the US ambassador to Japan, Joseph C. Grew, was somehow behind the confiscation, though Doyle never referred to the informal advice from the Army that spurred the action. Customs reiterated to the press that the consignees themselves had first called inspectors' attention to the novelette because it was "detrimental to Japanese-American relations."[12] However, despite Doyle and Moyle's deft spin control, a storm of public and political attention began building around the confiscated novelettes.

Honolulu Custom House. US Customs shared the building with a post office and courts. *Library of Congress (HABS HI-525)*

Honolulu Collector of Customs J. Walter Doyle, ca. 1926. Library of Congress (LC-B2-6217-1)

Honolulu was a Navy town, and Japanese Americans were upset that the novelette described US warships in great detail and seemed designed to stir a patriotic—anti-American—reaction from "the younger generation of Japanese." Indeed, it seemed that Japanese Americans were more indignant about the novelette than their Anglo neighbors. The very day after the *Hinode* seizure went public, Hawaiian editorials began questioning the absurdity of impounding a work of fiction. The Army intelligence officer at Fort Shafter wrote, "This is believed to be the first time that such a seizure of Japanese publications has been made here."[13] So far, only the customs clerk's wife, George Kojima, and a few dozen of his customers were familiar with the content of the novelette.

Word spread quickly about both the novelette and its seizure. On December 14, 1933, the Tokyo correspondent of the London *Morning Post* filed a story about the seizure, and the US military attaché in Great Britain, Lt. Col. Cortlandt Parker, made sure that Washington was advised.[14] Newspapers around the world picked up the story the next day.[15] Eleven days after the seizure, Los Angeles's recently elected Democratic congressman, Charles Colden, gently asked Secretary of War George Dern for information about the novelette. Dern replied that "the War Department has no official information whatever either of this pamphlet or of its seizure."[16] It was probably no coincidence that Fort Shafter typed up a detailed report for Washington on the very day of Colden's request. That some anonymous Army officer had only informally recommended that the book be seized allowed Secretary Dern to quibble about having "no official information"— not yet, at least. No federal executive in his right mind wanted to touch an explosive issue wired to national defense, international relations with Japan, and domestic race relations.

Seized Japanese Book
Reveals Propaganda for
War Against America

2327-H-36

Text Shows Intent to Strike First Blows at Our Bases in Philippines and Hawaii

SEES WAR WITH U. S.

(Copyright, 1934, by the Washington Herald and
Universal Service, Inc.)

The Washington Herald today publishes for the first time the first installment of a comprehensive and exclusive translation of the inflammatory pamphlet, "A Narrative of the Japanese-United States Future War," 1,250 copies of which were seized December 14, in Honolulu, by U. S. customs officers.

This treatise, thinly disguised as a novel, was written by a retired Japanese naval officer, and outlines methods to be employed in waging and winning a war with the United States.

It carries the unqualified indorsements of Admiral Kanji Kato, councilor of military affairs, and of Vice Admiral Nobumasa Suetsugu, chief of naval operations of Japan, who only a few days ago in Tokyo declared war with the United States is inevitable.

SABOTAGE SUGGESTED

Veritable handbooks of sedition and suggestion of ways and means to commit sabotage in this country and its possessions, the books are being closely held, and except for the translation the Herald has obtained, there are not known to be any others outside of official sources here.

Officials who have read the translation say it is startling in its accuracy, and in the semiofficial tone of its suggestions.

Since the contents of the so-called "dream novel" became known protests have been made privately by the State Department to the Japanese foreign office. It is learned officials in Tokyo merely shrugged their shoulders, so to speak, and pointed out the author of the book is not an active naval officer, but a retired one.

CALL IT "DREAM NOVEL"

Furthermore, they pointed out, it is merely a "dream novel," as the author explains, and no officers of the navy would think of doing what is pointedly suggested in the little handbook of violence.

Full of obvious substitutions, such as the use of the word "Negroes" where "Filipinos" or "Japanese" are plainly in-→

VICE ADMIRAL SUETSUGU

Vice Admiral Suetsugu on front page of *Washington Herald*, 1934.
Photo by author, National Archives RG 165, MID 2327-H-36/11

On January 15, 1934, a Hearst newspaper in the nation's capital, the *Washington Herald*, ran a front-page article about Fukunaga's novelette. The subtitle warned, "Text Shows Intent to Strike First Blows at Our Bases in Philippines and Hawaii." The warning was no surprise to US Navy strategists but would be forgotten by the public for another eight years. The *Herald* published a "comprehensive and exclusive translation" of Fukunaga's book, which was probably leaked by someone at the US Military Intelligence Division. Japanese vice admiral Nobumasa Suetsugu, commander of the Imperial Japanese Navy, glared at readers from a large photograph on the *Herald*'s front page. Commander Fukunaga may have penned the novelette, but Vice Admiral Suetsugu and his colleague, Admiral Kanji Kato, surely inspired it.

PACIFIC POWER STRUGGLE

Admiral Kato and Vice Admiral Suetsugu roused the Imperial Japanese Navy against the US Navy in the early 1930s, but, ironically, the Imperial Japanese Navy owed its modern awakening to an intrusion by the US Navy in 1853. The catalyst of that awakening was the violation of Japanese waters by an aggressive flotilla commanded by Commodore Matthew Perry. He was the envoy of a fledgling American republic less than a hundred years old, determined to force friendship and commercial treaties upon an ancient, reclusive society more than two thousand years old. The upstart US had expanded to the Pacific coast only three years prior.

Shaken by the insidious encroachment of Western imperialism into East Asia, Japan was determined to adapt to modern rules of geopolitical competition to survive. Japan had kept Dutch, Portuguese, and other Western traders at arm's length for two centuries until 1854, when Commodore Perry pushed an American friendship treaty upon the shogunate at gunpoint. Jolted by the humiliating subjugation and dismemberment of China and Southeast Asia by Europeans in the mid-nineteenth century, Japan embraced frenzied modernization to resist Western domination. The frantic process caused Japan to endure tumultuous political change and social disruption, and she not only rose to the challenges presented by British, French, Russian, Dutch, and American colonial expansion, but Japan would become an international competitor herself by the turn of the century.

New naval technologies shrank distances between the growing navies of Japan and the US. The Pacific rivalry germinated long before it came into public view. As far back as 1889, the US Office of Naval Intelligence (ONI) chief in London, F. E. Chadwick, tried to purchase blueprints of a Japanese cruiser being constructed in British shipyards. In 1890, ONI began tracking all Japanese naval officers who visited the US. Nevertheless, US intelligence was hobbled by American puritanical perceptions of spying as evil, while military and naval officers avoided intelligence assignments as career dead ends. Accordingly, intelligence budgets were insufficient to keep up with events.[17] The US victory in the Spanish-American War in 1898 increased friction between the nascent world powers.

The *Stars and Stripes* sprouted provocatively across the Pacific, on Alaska's Aleutian Islands in 1867, then on the islands of Hawaii, American Samoa, Guam, and the Philippines by 1899. Christian missionaries from the US drove deeper into China, proselytizing for democracy and human rights while they saved souls, and US railroad companies sniffed at business opportunities in Manchuria. US inroads in Asia aroused Japanese vigilance and spurred Tokyo to lay the ground for geostrategic countermoves and to expand her naval and military forces. If a new American republic could compete with the European empires, then so could Japan. By the turn of the twentieth century, Japan was anxious to expand her own realm.

In 1895, Japan stripped China of regional dominance—and the island of Taiwan—with victory in the First Sino-Japanese War. Great Britain joined Japan in an alliance in 1902 that acknowledged Japan's growing power and enhanced the relationship with British advisors and sales of modern warships. Three years later, Admiral Heihachiro Togo's adept naval victory at Tsushima Straits secured victory in the Russo-Japanese War, dispelling notions of European superiority, establishing Japan among the top tier of imperial powers, changing the balance of power in the Far East, and giving Japan half of Russia's Sakhalin Island, footholds in China's Manchuria, and a sphere of influence in Korea. Japan would soon take advantage of the latter to subvert and subjugate Korea in 1910.

Regardless of these prizes, the Japanese public was incensed by the Treaty of Portsmouth, which settled the Russo-Japanese War. Some activists had unreal expectations of victorious booty—Manchuria's Liaodong Peninsula, a piece of the Russian Far East, and a huge, punitive indemnity from Russia's treasury. They accused the treaty arbitrator, Theodore Roosevelt, of cheating Japan of her rightful spoils of war. When the treaty terms were announced on September

Victorious Japanese soldiers on parade in Tokyo after the Russo-Japanese War, 1905. *Naval Historical Center (NH 101541)*

A Japanese victory parade in Yokohama, 1905. *Naval Historical Center (NH 101543)*

5, 1905, a mob 30,000 strong rampaged through Tokyo for two days, attacking the Ministry of Foreign Affairs, police stations, American diplomatic and missionary facilities, and more than three hundred other buildings. Instead of victory parades, riots and protests ignited in other cities, and martial law was declared to calm the streets. Few Japanese realized that, despite their resounding victories at Tsushima Straits, Port Arthur, Mukden, and elsewhere in Manchuria, Japanese forces were stretched to their limits, and Japan's economy lacked the depth or deep pockets to sustain a protracted war.

Puck magazine mocked racist immigration policy that banned Japanese but allowed European extremists, March 13, 1907. *Library of Congress (AP101.P7 1907, Case X)*

Japanese in Honolulu cheer Emperor Taisho (Yoshihito (1879-1926), Hirohito's father) in a celebration on January 20, 1916. By 1933, Japanese immigrants and their descendants made up one-third of Hawaii's population. *Library of Congress (LC-USZ62-98385)*

Japanese rage was amplified by popular perceptions that Western prejudice against Asians shortchanged Japan in her due rewards for total victory over Russia. American prejudice was real enough to prompt the 1907 Gentlemen's Agreement, whereby Japan would impede immigration of her citizens to the US, and the US would refrain from imposing formal immigration restrictions against Japanese newcomers. The informal agreement did not end widespread racial discrimination against the 30,000 Japanese already in mainland US states and catered to the racist demands of a vocal Asian exclusion movement. Meanwhile, many US newspapers eagerly fomented "Yellow Peril" hysteria, conjuring up images of morally degenerate Asian hordes invading the US. Japanese leaders were rightfully incensed by the US attitudes but were oblivious to their own self-perceptions of racial superiority over Chinese, Koreans, and other Asian nationalities.

In August 1914, Japan unhesitatingly joined her British ally in war against the Central Powers. Japan conquered German colonial possessions in China and the Pacific. By the end of the First World War, Japanese destroyers and cruisers patrolled the Mediterranean Sea and Indian Ocean, Japanese products enjoyed great demand from European Allies and neutrals, and Japanese intelligence services extended operations into South Asia and Latin America.

The Imperial Japanese Navy became a potent instrument for protecting Japanese sovereignty and projecting Japan's power far beyond her shores.

The US grew wary of the Japanese competition. Details of provocative incidents were often kept mum by elite circles in the Departments of State, War, and Navy. In 1902, American soldiers found the body of a Japanese general staff officer among dead guerrillas after an engagement on Luzon. At a 1911 state banquet in Mexico City, the grand admiral of the Japanese Fleet was jubilantly toasted with rousing cheers of *"Viva Japón! Abajo los gringos!"* (Down with the gringos!). Four years later, the Japanese armored cruiser *Asama* ran aground at Puerto San Bartolome, Baja California, 300 miles south of San Diego, while searching for German cruisers SMS *Dresden* and SMS *Prinz Eitel Friederich*. US newspapers howled that the Japanese cruiser and a number of support vessels were landing spies and surveying isolated harbors and coastline, although a 15-meter gash through *Asama*'s hull from an uncharted rock clearly showed that the event was an accident.[18]

Germany and Mexico appealed to Japan's rancor against the US to entice Japan to abandon the Allies, ca. 1917. *Library of Congress (CAI-Rogers, W.A. no. 302)*

Nevertheless, American paranoia of Japan cast long shadows of doubt over *Asama*'s predicament.

During the Mexican Revolution, Japan quietly gave military assistance to various anti-US factions—50,000 rifles to the reactionary General Victoriano Huerta in 1913, then provided military equipment and advisors to Huerta's adversary, revolutionary First Chief Venustiano Carranza, in 1916. Huerta and Carranza were ideological opposites, but Japanese diplomats recognized that both were staunch nationalists willing to defy the US. In June 1916, Japanese commandos began participating in cross-border raids against military and civilian targets in Texas in a secret campaign of terror under the aegis of Carranza's Plan of San Diego. The Japanese-Mexican-German alliance proposed by the Zimmermann telegram a few months later was not merely a German fantasy. In February 1917, Japan sent engineers and machinery to construct a munitions plant in Carranza's Mexico. Even though Japan was waging war against the Central Powers in Europe and Asia, Austro-Hungarian and German expatriates facilitated the logistics and construction of the Japanese enterprise. Rivalry between Japan and the US soon faded in Mexico but intensified elsewhere around the Pacific.

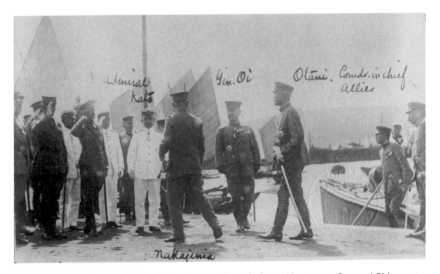

Allied officers salute as Admiral Kato (*center*, in white) and Lieutenant General Shigemoto Oi welcome General Masatake Nakajima and General Kikuzo Otani in Vladivostok, 1918. *Library of Congress (LC-B2-5037-2)*

Admiral Kato's battleships *Asahi* and *Iwami* in Vladivostok harbor in early 1918 (*center*). HMS *Suffolk* is at left. *Naval Historical Center (NH 50290)*

Battleships *Asahi* and *Iwami*

The 1918 entry of Japanese battleships *Asahi* and *Iwami* into Vladivostok, Russia's principal Pacific port, was symbolic. Both ships saw combat in the Russo-Japanese War; however, *Iwami* fought as the Russian battleship *Orel* and surrendered to Japan at Tsushima in May 1905. As a result of the 1922 Washington Naval Conference, *Asahi* was converted to a transport/repair ship and *Iwami* was scrapped and sunk as a naval aircraft target in 1924. *Asahi* was sunk in 1942 by US submarine *Salmon*.

Japanese and American infantrymen patrol the Trans-Siberian Railroad during a fractious partnership in the Russian Far East, November 12, 1918. *National Archives (111-SC-75288)*

Tense encounters with the sharp tendrils of Japanese political, intelligence, and military expansion became more frequent as the US presence increased in the Far East. As the First World War waned, doughboys of the American Expeditionary Force–Siberia had several confrontations with their supposed Japanese allies in Manchuria and the Russian Far East. In June 1919, a small detachment of the US 27th Infantry weathered a volatile Mexican standoff against a superior force of Japanese troops and Russian-Buryat Mongol Cossacks at Verkhne-Udinsk (now Ulan Ude), a town on the Trans-Siberian Railroad just east of Lake Baikal.[19] Upon their return to the US, veterans of the Siberian campaign appeared before congressional committees and American Legion conventions to rehash firsthand accounts of widespread Japanese hostility.

Japanese delegates to Paris Peace Conference in 1919, *left to right:* Baron Nobuaki Makino, Hikokichi Ijuin (ambassador to Italy), Prince Kinmochi Saionji, Matsui Keishiro (ambassador to France) and Viscount Sutemi Chinda (ambassador to Great Britain). *Library of Congress (LC-B2-4921-7)*

Japan's contributions to Allied victory over the Central Powers in the First World War earned her major power status. Japanese diplomats took their place alongside representatives of European empires and American republics at the Paris Peace Conference. Their active role in the Versailles Treaty and the flurry of other treaties and international conferences marked Japan's entry into the exclusive club of dominant powers. However, the Japanese soon came to the bittersweet realization that the Western powers did not really regard them as equals, especially when a "racial equality clause" in the Covenant of the League of Nations was rejected by the British and Americans.

RADICALS INCENSED BY RATIOS

The 1921–22 Washington Naval Conference intended to relieve tension in East Asia. However, many Japanese naval leaders felt slighted by the resulting disarmament agreement, which set a 5:5:3 ratio in capital ships of Great Britain, the US, and Japan. Japanese planners insisted that their future victory demanded a fleet that was at least 70 percent the size of the US Navy's combined Pacific and Atlantic fleets. Japan's delegation leader, Navy minister Admiral Tomosaburo Kato, realized that Japan did not have the industrial or economic power to compete with the US in an arms race, so he agreed to the 5:5:3 ratio. Admiral Kato's naval aide in Washington, Admiral Kanji Kato, president of Japan's Naval War College, adamantly opposed the ratio, which was codified into the Five Power Treaty. The resulting disagreement about the capital ships ratio in Washington caused a schism in the Imperial Japanese Navy that would even destabilize domestic politics in Japan—and eventually inspire a reserve commander to pen *Account of the Future US-Japan War*.

The Washington Naval Conference in 1922, where international limits on battleship construction aimed to prevent an arms race between major powers. The Japanese delegation sits at bottom left. *Library of Congress (LC-H27-A-4041)*

Admiral Kanji Kato (*left front*) stands with Lieutenant General Giichi Tanaka at the Washington Naval Conference, ca. 1922. *Library of Congress (LC-F8-16466)*

Spying at the Washington Naval Conference
Nine years after the conference, Japanese diplomats and admirals were shocked to learn that cryptanalysts of US signals intelligence were intercepting their secret communications with Tokyo to sneak a peek at Japan's negotiating position. However, the spying was not so one-sided. On the eve of the conference, US intelligence determined that Japan had secret sources of information in Congress and the White House, as well as paid agents of influence in the US and British presses.[20]

The officer corps of the Imperial Japanese Navy polarized into two opposing factions, which were mirrored by supporting civilian political groups both public and secret. The Treaty Faction (*Jōyaku-ha*) supported disarmament, was championed by pragmatists in the Navy Ministry, and was associated with liberalism and the civilian—democratic—government. The Fleet Faction (*Kantai-ha*) vociferously railed against the Five Power Treaty ratio as an affront and a threat to Japan. Followers rallied behind Admiral Kato and were supported by ultranationalists in the Imperial Japanese Army. The treaty debate drove a sharp bloody wedge into Japanese politics as the Fleet Faction and its militarist allies acted with increasing violence to silence or eliminate Treaty Faction opponents.

Japanese politics of the 1920s embroiled a dangerous chemistry, brewing volatile, insoluble elements of modern liberal democracy with traditionalist values. A nationwide bank failure in 1927 prefaced the Great Depression in 1930, and the twin disasters devastated farms, small businesses, and medium-sized firms "to the advantage of the *zaibatsu*—the great financial and industrial empires" of Mitsubishi, Mitsui, Sumitomo, and other conglomerates that bankrolled major political parties.[21] Many liberal politicians advocated arms control for budgetary reasons—the mountains of yen that were pumped into shipyards, aircraft factories, and other defense industries could have been injected into the economy elsewhere. However, these moderating voices were the targets of militarist fanatics belonging to scores of secret ultranationalist societies who ignited competing campaigns of intimidation and assassination in the early 1920s.

Traditional beliefs and modern ideologies mixed into combustible mindsets among the ranks. State Shinto appropriated traditional beliefs to institutionalize imperial boosterism throughout every Japanese community from metropolis to village. Most military officers had roots among the rural families impoverished by the recent financial calamities. Radical political and economic ideas took root among junior army officers and in due course spread into the navy. Some young warriors schemed to implement a Showa Restoration—a "state socialism administered by military dictatorship," whereupon the *zaibatsu* would surrender their vast fiefdoms to the Emperor Showa (also known as Hirohito), and the parliamentary political parties would likewise surrender their power to the sovereign.[22] The emperor was not consulted by or even sympathetic with the fanatics plotting assassinations and coups in his name, but a uniquely Japanese form of militarism in his name took root in the restive ranks.

In comparison to their radical Army brethren, officers of the Imperial Japanese Navy were conservative.[23] "The Navy disliked both the extreme nationalist wing of the Army and the secret military police [of the Kempeitai]" but had a weakness for its own dissident Fleet Faction.[24]

The 1930 London Naval Treaty aimed at world disarmament but ignited a firestorm in Japan that would eventually help kindle a world war. In the US, Great Britain, and France, only admirals, treasury officials, and shipbuilding communities took interest. In Japan, the treaty garnered daily headlines and became a highly delicate matter that threatened to destabilize the fragile relationship between nascent democratic institutions and the military establishment. The conferees in London hoped to limit cruisers, submarines, and other warships not restricted by the Washington agreement.

Meanwhile, a vicious disagreement in the Japanese government deepened the schism between the Treaty Faction and the Fleet Faction in the Cabinet, Foreign Ministry, *Kizoku-in* (the House of Peers of the Imperial Diet), Privy Council, political parties, Army, and, of course, Navy. The Fleet Faction was incensed by foreign attempts to thwart Japanese ambitions in East Asia and the Pacific. Paradoxically, the London Naval Treaty invigorated the Fleet Faction extremists.

A resolute prime minister, Osachi Hamaguchi, labored mightily to have the London treaty ratified as one of many austerity measures when the shadow of the Great Depression swept over Japan. *Time* magazine reported the international perception of the Treaty Faction principles in June 1930:

It was clear to him [Hamaguchi], as it certainly is clear to all Occidental experts, that Japan obtains great advantages from the Treaty, although naturally not getting all she asked in every category. Lumping her gains together it appears that while she set out to get 70% of the US naval strength in battleships, cruisers, destroyers, and submarines, she got 71.3%. Therefore, the lion-hearted Prime Minister ignored all protests, bloody or otherwise, prepared to push ratification of the Treaty.[25]

Hamaguchi's victory would be short-lived, and it caused his life to be cut short as well. On November 14, 1930, a twenty-one-year-old ultranationalist shot Hamaguchi in the stomach as he boarded a train in Tokyo Station. The elderly prime minister survived the assassination attempt but lost his political momentum as well as 11 inches of his intestines. In April 1931, Hamaguchi and his entire cabinet resigned, and he died four months later.

Osachi Hamaguchi, fervent supporter of London Naval Treaty, stands with his cabinet, December 1929. *Left to right:* Prime Minister Hamaguchi; Under-Secretary for Finance Gotaro Ogawa; Army Minister General Kazushige Ugaki, who did not cooperate with ultranationalists but also did not punish them; Foreign Minister Baron Kijuro Shidehara, who boldly advocated pacifism, nonintervention in China, and friendly relations with USA and Great Britain; Supreme War Council member Admiral Keisuke Okada, who narrowly missed assassination in 1936. *Library of Congress (LC-B2-6363-6)*

Meanwhile, the Fleet Faction received a boost from an unexpected source—an American intelligence veteran's book. In June 1931, Herbert O. Yardley, the recently laid-off chief of US codebreakers, published the book *American Black Chamber*. It boasted of peacetime intelligence-gathering exploits against Japan during the 1922 Washington Naval Conference and throughout the 1920s. By the time Japan's Kwantung Army invaded Manchuria in September 1931, Yardley's exposé was a best seller in Tokyo as well as in New York.[26]

The Fleet Faction lent the Army's ultranationalists a veneer of respectability. In contrast to the radical junior officers buzzing around the Army's secret hives of firebrands, the naval officer corps was conservative, comfortable with international commerce and the *zaibatsu*, and less xenophobic.

However, the Fleet Faction felt that the ratios set by both naval treaties were brazen insults to Japan's prestige. The London agreement radicalized the Fleet Faction.[27]

In 1932, the Fleet Faction inspired a group of junior naval officers to force their way into the residence of Prime Minister Tsuyoshi Inukai to stage the seminal "May 15 incident." They shouted down Inukai's exhortation for dialogue, then shot the seventy-seven-year-old statesman to death. The assassins took taxis to the police station, turned themselves in, and made their trial a political platform. Like most other rightwing assassins in prewar Japan, popular support garnered them light sentences. From that time until the attack on Pearl Harbor in 1941, Japan marched resolutely into a period that would become known as "the dark valley" (*kurai tanima*), where liberalism withered in the shadows of ultranationalism and militarism. Inukai's brutal assassination marked the end of Japan's civilian rule until 1946. It also signaled the ascent of Fleet Faction leaders such as Admiral Kato and Vice Admiral Suetsugu.

INCENDIARY ENDORSEMENTS

Account of the Future US-Japan War was indeed unique among war fiction of the day. It was blessed with two unusual forewords, one written by Admiral Kanji Kato, member of Japan's Supreme War Council, and another by Vice Admiral Nobumasa Suetsugu. Both men believed that war with the US was inevitable.

Vice Admiral Suetsugu recommended the book for "the general public as well as naval specialists" because of the astute glimpses it afforded of future warfare. No one was more qualified to give such a recommendation. Suetsugu was the fifty-two-year-old son of a samurai, a graduate of the Imperial Japanese Naval Academy, a renowned tactician and submarine commander, and a veteran of the Russo-Japanese War and the First World War. While serving as naval attaché to Great Britain in 1916, he observed the Battle of Jutland from the bridges of Royal Navy warships.[28] In 1921, he accompanied the Japanese delegation to the arms limitation conference in Washington and afterward became a prominent proponent of the Fleet Faction, which vociferously opposed the restrictions of the 1922 Washington Naval Treaty and the 1930 London Naval Treaty. During high-level staff assignments, Suetsugu devised battle plans for the next war in the Pacific. As head of the Navy General Staff's operational planning section from 1922 to 1925, Suetsugu refined the strategy of interceptive operations—*yōgeki sakusen*, which aimed to destroy the US Pacific Fleet in one epic decisive battle in Japanese waters á la Tsushima Strait 1905. "*Yōgeki sakusen*, essentially a strategy of attrition, became naval orthodoxy during the 1930s," wrote historian John Stephan.[29] And *yōgeki sakusen* laid the foundation of Fukunaga's fictional plot.

In his preface to Fukunaga's book, Admiral Suetsugu claimed to have "read this story through without once laying the book aside." Indeed, it would not be a surprise if Suetsugu and Kato had dictated the plotline to the author. Kato also praised Fukunaga's book for emphasizing the "great importance that control of the air bears to national defense." Although Kato was an old salt with more than four decades under his belt, he had a keen understanding of new technologies and their potential applications, and he realized Japan's need for a modern naval air arm to defeat the US in the Pacific. Indeed, Kato's avid embrace of new technology and his international experience belied criticism that he was a feudal throwback, like some of the militarists in army circles who aspired to regress to samurai days. Fukunaga's novelette could not have been blessed with a more prestigious, forward-looking endorsement.

Kanji Kato was one of the visionaries and architects of Japan's modern navy. He had served in most every major training and command position the service could offer: naval attaché to Great Britain, commandant of the Naval Academy at Etajima, chief of the gunnery school, president of the Naval War College, chief and vice chief of the naval general staff, commander in chief of the Combined Fleet, and member of the Supreme Military Council. War was no stranger to Kato, who blazed a distinguished record in every Japanese conflict since the 1895 Sino-Japanese War. He was chief gunner on battleship *Mikasa* in the Russo-Japanese War. During World War I, Kato commanded a destroyer squadron in the Mediterranean that escorted Australian and New Zealand Army Corps (ANZAC) troopships in joint operations with the Royal Navy.[30] In January 1918, Kato led battleships *Asahi* and *Iwami* into Vladivostok harbor as the spearhead of the Allied intervention in the Russian Far East.

Like many of his counterparts in the US Navy, Kato was convinced that America and Japan were destined to become enemies in the Pacific. As a young officer he had witnessed the US takeover of the Hawaiian Islands. Kato had once "expressed regret that Japan did not intervene in Hawaii during the 1893 revolution."[31] His encounters with American naval and military forces in Siberia and Manchuria between 1918 and 1920 reinforced his belief that the US would be an impediment to Japanese expansion. When Kato visited Washington in 1921 for the naval conference, he could not have avoided exposure to the caustic public debate about Asian immigrants—especially Japanese (a prologue to the fervidly anti-Asian Immigration Act of 1924).[32]

Admiral Kato's disgust with the naval treaties intensified in 1931, when Herbert Yardley revealed that US codebreakers eavesdropped on confidential Japanese communications during the 1921–22 disarmament conference. The admiral may not have been surprised to discover that the British also peeked at the Japanese cards during the 1930 conference. Incidentally, "the Japanese traffic was a sparkling success" for the codebreakers of the British Government Code and Cypher School (GCCS).[33] Perhaps it was no coincidence that Admiral Kato's nephew, Hideya Morikawa, became a trailblazer of Japanese cryptanalysis, building the secret Special Section (*Tokumu Han*) of the naval general staff's communication department into a formidable signals intelligence organization.[34]

Kato's public opposition to the disarmament agreements grew after the London Naval Treaty. He gave the pro-treaty Navy minister, Takeshi Takarabe, the cold shoulder. When Minister Takarabe paid Kato a courtesy call soon after returning to Japan, "the call lasted the bare five minutes etiquette demanded." Soon after, in May 1930, the admiral declined the invitation of the America-Japan Society to a farewell banquet for US ambassador William R. Castle Jr. Around that time, Kato's protégé, Lieutenant Commander Yeiji Kusakari, a promising forty-year-old officer with four children, committed ritual suicide—*seppuku*—on a night train to Tokyo. The act was immediately attributed to the Fleet Faction and Kato.[35] Meanwhile, Kato discarded his lifelong stoicism to vociferously condemn the 1930 treaty. Observers speculated that Kato's unusual behavior was "brought about by the machinations of a wily subordinate, Admiral Suetsugu."[36] In 1934, Admiral Kato became head of the Imperial Japanese Navy after Treaty Faction leaders were forced to resign. He appointed Vice Admiral Suetsugu commander of Japan's Combined Fleet. The Fleet Faction took control of the navy and set a course for war with the US.

Kyosuke Fukunaga, the author of *Account of the Future US-Japan War*, was a naval officer, scholar, and writer. He was born in 1889 in Tokyo and was a 1908 graduate of the thirty-sixth class of the Imperial Japanese Naval

著 者

Kyosuke Fukunaga, lieutenant commander (retired), Imperial Japanese Navy, ca. 1933. *University of Maryland, Prange collection*

Academy at Etajima, alongside many future Fleet Faction admirals. Of the 191 midshipmen in Fukunaga's class, at least fifty-one rose to flag rank: three were destined to be full admirals, fifteen to be vice admirals, and thirty-three to be rear admirals. One of his classmates was Admiral Chuichi Nagumo, who would command the attacks on Pearl Harbor in 1941 and Midway Island in 1942. In 1918, Fukunaga retired from active duty but remained in the reserves and held the rank of lieutenant commander when he published *Account of the Future US-Japan War* in 1933.

An intellectual as well as a naval officer, Fukunaga published at least two books that offered scholarly insight into the Japanese language. In 1926, he contributed to efforts to reform and modernize Japanese written language with a tome titled *National Language and Script Problem* (*Kokugo*

Japanese War Fantasy

Vice Admiral Chuichi Nagumo, a prominent Fleet Faction leader and commander of the 1941 Pearl Harbor attack, was a classmate of Kyosuke Fukunaga at the Imperial Japanese Naval Academy. *Naval Historical Center (NH 63423)*

kokuji mondai). On the eve of World War II, he coauthored *Dictionary of Spoken Language* (*Kogo jiten*), which cataloged "simpler colloquial equivalents for literary words, in particular words borrowed from the Chinese language."[37]

Fukunaga was a versatile writer who had the technical expertise to give casual readers perceptive insights into the strategy, tactics, and weaponry of modern warfare. One of his first books was *The Story of Warships for Children* in 1932. After *Account of the Future US-Japan War* in 1933, he authored *Shanghai Land Battle Corps* in 1938, *The Nation's Defense* (*Kuni no mamori*) in 1939, a book about submarine warfare in 1942, and *Kaisho Arai Ikunosuke*, a 1943 biography about a Tokugawa-era samurai who became navy minister in 1869, and he also wrote one of the first English-Japanese dictionaries.[38]

Fukunaga's 1933 novelette opened a keyhole view into the thoughts of his mentors, the extremists in the Imperial Japanese Navy who were tacking toward war with the US. His voice reflected the radicalism that transformed Japan from a budding liberal democracy to a militarist dictatorship. In the years to come, the extremism accelerated the pace of assassinations, silencing most moderate voices in Japanese politics. Of Japan's sixteen prime ministers between the world wars, five were assassinated. Prestige, power, and popularity protected no one from assassination in Japan. When the heretofore conservative Navy tacked toward extremism, the nation followed. Alas, Fukunaga would live to see the defeat and humiliation that his mentors wrought, but he would also bear witness to Japan's remarkable recovery before he died in 1971.

Admiral Suetsugu, Fukunaga's mentor, became Japan's "most notable 'political' naval officer" in the late 1930s. Acclaimed foreign policy analyst John Gunther wrote, "He [Suetsugu] was the most Fascist-inclined man in Japan; it was he who created the 'ideological squads' to rout out 'dangerous thinkers.'"[39] Historian Gordon Prange was more succinct: "Suetsugu was the navy's number one fire breather."[40] A 1934 article by Suetsugu in the popular magazine *Gendai* accused Charles Lindbergh of being a US spy after bad weather grounded the famous aviator's 1931 East Asian tour in the disputed Kurile Islands.[41] By late 1938, Suetsugu was not only spear-heading Japan's campaign to attack and occupy Canton (modern Guangzhou), China's major port, but also leading the "ultra-chauvinistic element in the Government" (in the words of US ambassador Joseph Grew).[42] His prominence garnered him the post of home minister in the cabinet of Prime Minister Fumimaro Konoye during the heady months when the National Mobilization Law imposed a state of emergency and war economy throughout Japan. However, Suetsugu was too autocratic even for a Japan with war fever. His "extremist views in advocating the creation of a single national party and drastic measures along totalitarian lines" precipitated the resignation of Konoye and his cabinet in January 1939.[43] By that time, Suetsugu, Kato and Fukunaga had each done their parts to push Japan into world war.

Regrettably, Admiral Kato did not witness the misery that his pro-war legacy wrought upon Japan. He died of a cerebral hemorrhage at his seaside villa in February 1939. By that time, Suetsugu was already the standard bearer of the navy's hawks. Despite making public statements supporting the banishment of whites from Asia, Suetsugu seemed to be a darling of Nazi correspondents in Tokyo.[44] Had he not died of natural causes in December 1944, he would have been tried as a war criminal.[45]

"Man-o'-War Row" in Shanghai, ca. 1935. Cruisers, gunboats, merchantmen, and other vessels from several nations crowd the Huangpu River. *"Naval Historical Center (NH S-502.01 Brian Jeffcott collection)*

FORECASTS AND FANTASY

"Kitarubeki monoga kita"—the inevitable has come—begins the first chapter. Fukunaga's fictional war ignites when a Japanese destroyer commanded by a hotheaded Japanese militarist pumps three torpedoes into USS *Houston*

in a brazen, unprovoked attack while the US warship sits anchored off Shanghai. The lieutenant responsible for this international incident is hauled back to Japan and court-martialed under the world's gaze, but three volleys from a firing squad whizz harmlessly past him, and the public hails the lieutenant as a national hero. The US demands reparations, and the crisis prompts the installation of a new hawkish cabinet in Tokyo, which expels the US ambassador and declares war on the US, where Japanese are being lynched in California streets. Events unfold to Fukunaga's readers between realistic scripts of radio broadcasts and dialogue between Japanese technicians in Manchuria. Fukunaga's drama foretold aspects of the future world war with techno-thriller style.

One American reader, Major Edward F. Witsell, devoured the book. Maj. Witsell was a 1911 graduate of the Citadel who had served two tours in Japan at the US embassy and was one of the few Japanese linguists in the US Army. He recommended that the Army chief of staff read a few choice passages "of military interest" in the novelette, starting with a description of Japan's rapid thrusts at Guam, the Philippines, and Hawaii.

Edward F. Witsell
Maj. Witsell was a 1911 graduate of the Citadel who served as assistant US military attaché in Tokyo in 1922 alongside two other assistant attachés with successful intelligence careers ahead of them: Sydney F. Mashbir and Ellis M. Zacharias. In 1945, Witsell was appointed adjutant general of the Army, a distinguished position that gave him the dubious honor of signing thousands of telegrams informing families that their loved ones had been killed or gone missing in action. He retired in 1951 with the rank of major general.

To modern-day readers, there is an eerie familiarity to names and places in Fukunaga's narrative of the fantasy war in the Pacific. In Fukunaga's fiction, Admiral Nagano directed battleships *Mutsu* and *Nagato* and other elements of the Japanese Fleet against a superior US armada that was stalked by Japanese I-type submarines as it emerged from Pearl Harbor. Japan's enormous battleships *Musashi* and *Yamato* did not appear in Fukunaga's tale because they were still on secret drawing boards. The drama was laced with heated dialogue on ships' bridges and in crews' quarters about the capabilities of torpedoes, antisubmarine mines, airships, gunnery angles and ranges, and actions with USS *Wyoming*, *Utah*, *Nevada*, and scores of other warships that would go down in history a decade later. In the end of Fukunaga's short, glorious war, Japanese naval aircraft disabled the US carriers *Lexington*, *Saratoga*, and *Ranger* and scored a decisive victory in a grand sea battle in the Bonin Islands.

Fukunaga's novelette laid bare the dreams of Japanese militarists. It made no secret of Japan's designs on China and the Russian Far East. In a fictional dialogue between patrons of a Japanese bathhouse, Fukunaga's characters casually dismissed the Red Army: "Russia? Oh, since year before last, our army has been prepared for war, and Russia knows it. They also know that if they make a move, they will lose the maritime provinces." The Soviets considered the novelette important enough to have the state military printing bureau translate and publish it in Russian in 1934. For some mysterious reason, the Soviets even translated Fukunaga into Armenian.[46]

The prevailing theme throughout Fukunaga's fantasy was that underdog Japan could outmaneuver and defeat the superior forces of the US through courage and guile. Meanwhile, the US would be disoriented by saboteurs, fifth columnists, racial strife, political apathy, and a thin-skinned distaste for any prolonged fight.

"Japanese spies are everywhere," mumbles the fictional captain of USS *Oklahoma* as it creeps through the Panama Canal toward the Pacific. Moments later, his ship's magazine detonates, sabotaged by a rebellious African American sailor to show solidarity for the progressive Japanese. Fukunaga really believed that downtrodden races looked to Japan to free them from white oppressors, recycling an opaque vision propagated by the 1916 Plan of San Diego (an anti-US scheme of the Mexican intelligence service with surreptitious Japanese support) and similar Japanese propaganda themes with racial overtones.[47]

The target audience of Fukunaga's novelette in Hawaii was no stranger to racial discrimination. Even though Hawaii's Japanese American community made up one-third of the territory's population, they were prohibited from joining private clubs, buying or leasing property in certain areas, or entering many beaches, restaurants, and other establishments. A white-dominated oligarchy controlled Hawaii's economy, politics, and high society. "It is our country's duty to stir up and incite the Japanese in Hawaii to attack the Americans there," declares one of Fukunaga's characters. Indeed, militarists hoped that Japanese expatriates and *Nisei* (offspring of first-generation immigrants) would join their compliant countrymen on the pro-war bandwagon. Fukunaga conjured up a scenario where two average young men of Japanese descent named George and Frank spontaneously decided to sabotage a naval airship near San Francisco.

In hindsight, the only remotely similar event was the Ni'ihau incident. In the days after the 1941 Pearl Harbor attack, three residents of Japanese descent helped a downed Zero pilot on the isolated Hawaiian island of Ni'ihau but met tragic ends at the hands of their native hostages.[48]

Fear of such Japanese sympathizers and fifth columnists led to the internment of Japanese Americans in the US. Lt. Gen. John L. DeWitt, commander of the IX Corps Area in California, convinced President Franklin Roosevelt that the loyalty of Japanese Americans was suspect and instigated the internment of 127,000 people from Pacific coast states. In contrast, only 2,000 of the 158,000 Japanese Americans in Hawaii were deemed suspicious enough to warrant internment, though the entire Hawaii Territory was under martial law throughout the war.[49] An estimated 2,000 to 7,000 *Nisei* did serve in the Japanese government and armed forces during the Second World War, many of them with mixed feelings if not involuntarily. On the other hand, most Japanese Americans seemed skeptical of the orchestrated, jingoistic propaganda that emanated from Japan, which sympathized with militarist assassins, soft-pedaled military aggression in China, and promoted self-sacrifice as a patriotic calling. More than 30,000 Japanese Americans served in the US armed forces. About 6,000 *Nisei* worked as translators and interpreters with the Military Intelligence Service in the Pacific and were crucial to the Allied victory.[50]

As enlightening as the novelette was of battlefield innovations, it was equally informative of dangerous misconceptions that predisposed Japanese hawks to the idea of an achievable victory in the Pacific. Fukunaga's plot was built upon the Fleet Faction's assumption that the navies would decide the war. Japanese submarines and destroyers attacking in the dead of night would chip away at the US Fleet until it entered a "strategic inner defense" area where battleships and aircraft from carriers and airfields would pounce for the final kill.[51] To accomplish these feats, Admiral Kato molded a generation of naval officers to push "fierce and relentless training, especially night training." Commanders and sailors would make up for their navy's technological deficits with Japanese fighting spirit—*yamato damashii*.[52] Japan would bet her future on a short, fast war.

Fukunaga's novelette was much more than the pulp fiction it appeared to be in American eyes. The *Nisei* who examined it realized that it was a powerful political statement, a rejection of diplomacy and treaties, a nationalistic endorsement of an arms race, ethnic cleansing, and war. Fukunaga's book was the Fleet Faction's sales pitch to Japanese Americans. It was ironic

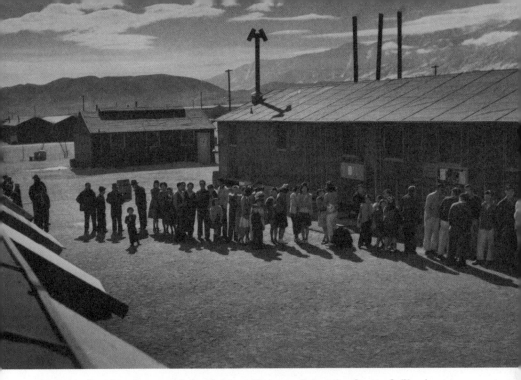

Japanese American internees in lunch line at Manzanar Relocation Center, California, ca. 1943. *Library of Congress (Ansel Adams LC-A35-6-M-22)*

that Japanese Americans brought it to the attention of US customs and the US Army because they worried that it would reflect poorly upon their community.

Alas, the greatest irony of Fukunaga's bombshell could not be realized until 1941 because that first volatile shipment of *Nichibei-sen Miraiki—Account of the Future US-Japan War*—dropped upon Honolulu's waterfront on December 7, 1933. The Japanese intention to attack Pearl Harbor and US interests throughout the Pacific was hardly any secret, as the 1933 novelette confirmed. The surprise lay merely in the date and execution.

****
****
****

ORIGINAL NOTES, FOREWORDS, AND PREFACE

NOTES BY US ARMY INTELLIGENCE

Notes by Far Eastern Section, G-2 (Army Intelligence)

The following pages contain a literal translation of the short story dealing with a future Japanese-American War, written by Lieutenant Commander Kyosuke Fukunaga, retired, Imperial Japanese Navy, that appeared as a supplement to the January 1934 number of *Hinode* Magazine published in Tokyo, Japan.

The first consignment of this supplement arrived in Honolulu on SS *President Taft* on December 7, 1933, consigned to George Kojima, the proprietor of a bookstore in Honolulu. The United States customs officials at Honolulu confiscated all copies of this supplement under Section 305 of the Tariff Act of 1930 and took similar action with respect to a similar consignment of the supplement that arrived in Honolulu on December 12, 1933, consigned to three Japanese stores in that city.

Section 305 of the Tariff Act of 1930, under which the seizure of this supplement was made, provides:

Sec. 305. Immoral Articles – Importation Prohibited.

(a) Prohibition of Importation. All persons are prohibited from importing into the United States from any foreign country any book, pamphlet, . . . or drawing containing any matter advocating or urging treason or insurrection against the United States or containing any threat to take the life of or inflict bodily harm upon any person in the United States."

Since the publication of this book, the Japanese government has taken steps to prevent the publication in the future of inflammatory books and articles presaging war and otherwise endangering relations with foreign countries.

Note by US Army G-2 Editor
Copies of the special New Year's edition of the magazine *Hinode*, together with the three large supplements thereto (of which this novel is one), are sold at the special price of 0.60 yen for the four volumes.

Note by US Army G-2 Translator
Words and phrases enclosed in brackets are supplied by the translator.

FOREWORDS BY IMPERIAL JAPANESE NAVY ADMIRALS

Foreword by Admiral Kanji Kato

As might have been expected, Mr. Fukunaga's fluent pen has well portrayed future warfare. I hope that this book will bring home to its readers the great importance that control of the air bears to national defense in this day and time.

Kanji Kato
Admiral, Imperial Japanese Navy, Member – Supreme Military Council
November 1933

Foreword by Vice Admiral Nobumasa Suetsugu

Mr. Kyosuke Fukunaga's *Account of the Future War between Japan and the United States* is extremely interesting to me by virtue of the fact that its author is a naval officer. I read this story through without once laying the book aside.

It is needless to say that it is most interesting as a novel, but what especially impressed me was the fact that although the author has been separated from active service for many years, he has such a complete knowledge of ever-developing modern naval tactics. Consequently, this book should be of interest to the general public as well as to naval specialists, particularly as it contains various hints [of what may be expected in such a war as the author depicts].

I greatly regret that, in view of my present position as commander of the Imperial Japanese Navy, I cannot express any exhaustive comments on this work because of the relation that exists between the contents thereof and military secrets. However, I believe that I can say this much with propriety: if we can be victorious in this way, it would indeed be delightful. Furthermore, any commander in chief who could have a man like Mr. Fukunaga as his chief of staff would indeed by very much heartened.

Nobumasa Suetsugu
Vice Admiral, Imperial Japanese Navy, Commander in Chief of the Grand Fleet

FUKUNAGA'S PREFACE

Do you mean to say that just because the United States Fleet appears to be on the verge of being ordered out of the Pacific Ocean there is no longer any reason to write an account of a future war between Japan and the United States? Don't joke about this matter. Do you really think that once the United States fleet is transferred to the Atlantic, it will remain nailed down there even until 1936?

Don't confuse a fleet with a fort.

The questions involved in writing *An Account of the Future War between Japan and the United States* present many very difficult problems. It is hard to say how many books on this subject have been published to the present time—not only in Japan, but in England, France, and Germany. Without exception, they have all been failures because they attempted to twist the truth to serve the ends of propaganda, or, like chewing old cud, have been overfilled with intricate details of strategy, or were merely foolish and melodramatic stories. For this reason, people are generally disgusted with such stories of a future Japan–United States war and regard them as trashy sensationalism.

This being the case, writing a story of this sort is, at the onset, beset with difficulties. In any account of what is to transpire in the future, it is most difficult to really convince your readers of the truth of your statements. Furthermore, as a rule, unless your story is sensational, it will fail to attract readers by its very innocuousness.

Nevertheless, I will attempt to undertake the difficult task of writing such a story. Whether or not my story of this future war will result in failure, as all others have, will depend, in the end, entirely on the judgment of my readers. I hope that either because of the pictures, or because of what is written, you will at least read one or two pages of this story before you reject it as just another visionary or foolish article.

I wish to apologize beforehand in one respect. This is what I mean: in the beginning of the story, the illegal sinking of an American warship by a Japanese destroyer is described. I personally do not believe that any officer of our present navy would be guilty of ordering such a rash act. I state this fact to protect the good name of Imperial Japanese Naval officers. Naturally, however, I personally can harbor such lawless ideas because I have long since been retired from active service due to physical disability.

Kyosuke Fukunaga
Author

CHAPTER 1
The Inevitable Happens

SECTION 1: WOOSUNG INCIDENT

"Say, radio man, have you repaired the wireless yet?"

The master, returning after a brief absence, thus questioned the repair man upon entering the disordered abode where benches, emery paper, rubber, guns, etc., were scattered about in disorder. He then slumped down in an easy chair.

The radio man, a youth of about 25 or 26 years of age, answered with a confused look. "Yes," he said, "I opened the transformer and replaced three tubes that I found to be defective. I also scraped the rust off the conductor."

"Exactly. It has been five years since we got this set," said the master, recalling as he spoke that with this combination radio and electric phonograph set they had quickly gotten the news about the famous May 15th Affair. "We bought this set from a salesman named Hashimura, didn't we? When we bought it, the salesman told us that we would be able to receive radio broadcasts from Japan without trouble."

"Well, I have fixed it so that we can get the broadcasts again," said the young mechanic as he looked at his wristwatch. "Wait a moment, the six o'clock broadcast will begin to come in shortly."

The scene above transpired in one of the houses of the South Manchuria Railway Company at Fuchimicho, Dairen in Manchuria. News broadcast in Japan at 7:00 p.m. Japan time is heard in Manchuria at 6:00 p.m. Manchuria time, the clocks in the latter place being one hour earlier than those in Japan.

Broadway Mansions, Shanghai's grandest apartment building, loomed over Suzhou Creek and the Garden Bridge and would soon become the headquarters of Japanese occupation, 1936. *Naval Historical Center (NH 81151)*

American destroyers USS *Paul Jones* (DD-230); USS *Pope* (DD-225), and USS *Parrott* (DD-218) (*left to right*). Shanghai, ca. 1936. *Naval Historical Center (NH 105794)*

Just then the pigeon in the upper part of the clock began to coo, and the mechanic twirling the receiving knob said, "That is Hiroshima broadcasting." Only a lot of noisy static could be heard. The mechanic protested, "I can't dial this static out."

"That's annoying," said the master with a black scowl. "When I bought that instrument the salesman told me that it was absolutely the best."

USS *Houston* in Manila, 1931. *Naval Historical Center (80-CF-21337-2)*

The two men stared at the cloth face of the receiver and strained their ears to listen to the announcer's voice. The static continued but faded, and the announcer's voice could now be heard more clearly, saying "... I repeat, as you have just been informed, today at 4:15 p.m., USS *Houston* of the United States Asiatic Fleet, while riding at anchor off Woosung [at Shanghai], was torpedoed and sunk by the Japanese navy destroyer *Nara*. The reason for this action is not clear. Order and quiet is being maintained aboard the American and Japanese naval craft anchored at Shanghai. Please stand by for further news that will be broadcast shortly."

USS *Houston* in Shanghai, 1933. *Naval Historical Center (NH 72460)*

USS *Houston*

USS *Houston* was a highly symbolic target for war fiction, having served as flagship of the US Asiatic Fleet from 1931 to 1933. In early 1931, war broke out between Japan and China, and *Houston* landed bluejackets at Shanghai to protect US interests. *Houston* paid a goodwill visit to Japan in May 1933. The real-life *Houston* sank with guns blazing at the Battle of Sunda Strait in March 1942.

IJN Destroyer *Nara*

Nara was launched in 1918, the lead ship of her destroyer class, but appears to have been reclassified as a minesweeper (*W-9*) by 1930 and was demilitarized ten years later.

Torpedomen on a Japanese destroyer prepare to fire at USS *Houston* during the Battle of Sunda Strait, March 1, 1942. *Naval Historical Center (SC 301085)*

The two listeners were astounded at the lack of concern with which the announcer broadcast the news of this important affair, which surely marked the very apex of a critical time. An American naval vessel had been sunk—by a Japanese warship!

"What? What's that? An American warship sunk?" The master was more frightened now than he had been five years previously when this same radio receiver had announced the assassination of the Japanese premier. The young mechanic was about to say something, but the master silenced him by raising his hand and saying, "Be quiet!"

"The next announcement will now be made . . ." the loudspeaker shouted. "Navy Department Announcement: According to the report of the commanding officer of the Third Imperial Naval Squadron, today at 3:00 p.m. the Imperial Naval destroyer *Nara* was en route from Shanghai to Hankow. At 3:45 p.m. the *Nara* arrived at the fortified harbor of Woosung, whereupon Lieutenant Eitaro Maki, commander of the destroyer *Nara*, entirely without orders or authority, fired two torpedoes at the flagship of the US Asiatic Fleet, USS *Houston*, which was anchored in that harbor.

These missiles struck their mark and caused the magazines of *Houston* to explode, with the result that the warship sank almost immediately. The water being shallow at this point, the cruiser was not completely submerged. *Nara* immediately cast off her small boats, but, despite every effort, the admiral commanding the *Houston* and 400 of her crew were lost. The commander of the Imperial Third Fleet immediately held a conference with the senior officer of the United States Fleet in Shanghai, and every effort is being exerted to prevent the outbreak of trouble. Lieutenant Maki, the offender, has been confined at the headquarters of the Third Fleet and is now undergoing an investigation. It may be added that Lieutenant Maki is the son of an army general who is at present a member of the Supreme Military Council."

This was a complete outline of the affair. However, for the two listeners in Dairen, it brought only great uneasiness. In truth, these two listeners realized, with Japanese intuition, the grave importance of the affair. There was no need to wait for further explanation by the announcer.

"This will develop into a serious matter, don't you think? It will bring about much trouble. The Japanese navy will . . ." mumbled the master, his mouth gaping as his words trailed off.

The young mechanic who had sat spellbound during the broadcast now exclaimed impulsively, "*Nara!* Destroyer commander Maki!"

"Do you know this unruly naval commander?" asked the master.

"No," answered the mechanic without hesitation, "but it seems to me that I have heard the name before."

"Anyway, it was a rash thing to do," said the master, pushing along the discussion with the mechanic to see what the young man knew about this Lieutenant Maki. "That fellow, the destroyer commander, sank a foreign naval vessel. Why, it is war . . ."

"No matter how they try to prevent it, war will result, don't you think?" replied the mechanic.

"Japan will have no say in the matter regardless of how much she wishes to prevent war. Remember the Spanish-American War? When something like this happened and an American warship was sunk in Cuba, it resulted in war," said the master, recalling an article he had read in the newspaper several days previously that reported riots in Cuba again.

The master was visibly upset. "I have heard recently that Japan will be confronted by a grave crisis in the year 1936. However, I didn't think that the crisis would happen so soon . . . Well, anyway, go over to the company office to see if you can get any further news."

The master rose to his feet while the mechanic put away his tools into a handbag and exited. Just then, the master's wife, who had entered the house from the back, came in and exclaimed, "I have just heard. Will this mean war?"

"I think so. I believe I will go over to the company office and ask what they think about it," said the master as he put on his hat.

"What radio store are you going to?" she inquired.

"To the radio shop in Tokiwacho, Yamano's radio shop."

SECTION 2: WOOSUNG AFTERMATH

In Japan, consternation reigned. Fearing the effect of the affair upon Japan's diplomatic relations, the foreign office and the navy department established rigid censorship over publication of any news connected with the *Houston* sinking. Nevertheless, the Japanese people were extremely apprehensive. Rumors and false reports flew fast and thick. Public feeling ran high. Small groups of seven or eight people gathered everywhere—in parks, on street corners, in the corners of cafes—and discussed the matter excitedly.

"Hasn't the United States demanded 2,000 billion dollars in reparations?"

"Converted into yen that would make 7,000 billion yen! Say!"

Reparations
2,000 billion dollars (i.e., 2 trillion dollars) in 1932 would be equivalent
to about 37 trillion dollars in 2021.

"America has demanded that Lieutenant Maki, the criminal, be delivered to her!"

"Perhaps they will lynch him when they get him?"

"Anyway, they say it is true that the government has humbly apologized to America."

"They say that the American newspapers state that the United States Fleet is being dispatched at once to kill off the Japanese."

"We have been greatly embarrassed by the reckless actions of the military both in this affair as well as in that of May 15th."

US sailors on shore leave, Chefoo (now Yantai), Shandong, China, 1936. *Naval Historical Center (NH 78369)*

"That first affair was a family quarrel and was all right, but this present matter is very different, being an issue between Japan and a foreign country!"

However, these discussions alone did not reveal the true sentiment of the Japanese people. Gathering courage from exponents of a strong policy, more and more people began to criticize the weak-kneed and timid policy of the government.

"The real cause of the affair was the jealousy that has long permeated the fleets of Japan and the United States at Shanghai. The fleets were always watching one another carefully, and the Japanese and American officers and sailors did nothing but fight when they encountered each other in the city on shore leave."

"It's said that Lieutenant Maki has escaped from jail in Shanghai."

"After escaping from jail, Lieutenant Maki has torpedoed the admiral's ship. Isn't that swell!"

"Don't believe what he says . . . If the fleet is dispatched, that will be only one move in this game, won't it? It's more important that we apologize for what has happened."

"Oh! Then I suppose that the United States Fleet will come to this part of the world to keep an eye on the doings of Lieutenant Maki."

While this wild talk, a mixture of hope and fear, was being bandied about, Lieutenant Maki was sent by warship from Shanghai to Yokosuka and brought to trial before a court martial. This action brought the wild rumors to an abrupt end because, even though the record of the preliminary investigation was secret, it became very clear to the large crowd attending the public hearing that no attempt was being made to conceal the true facts of the case.

Whether it was through fear of international consequences, or because the offense was so palpably simple, or because there were no accomplices to the offense, or because the investigating officials had so thoroughly performed their duty—the trial made good progress and opened at Yokosuka within one month of the offense. In addition to dispatching the chief of the personnel bureau of the navy department to act as president of the court martial, all the other members of the court were specially selected. The authorities exerted every effort to ensure that the trial would be properly conducted.

Gradually, as the trial progressed, the nation began to hear testimony about the defendant's daring and bravery. Furthermore, people were surprised that, despite the defendant's natural taciturnity, the taking of his testimony required two full days. Lieutenant Maki's testimony was essentially as follows:

"In the fall of last year (1935), everyone knows that the Second Washington Naval Conference, caused by the squabble over American and Japanese naval ratios decided at the First Washington Conference, resulted in a complete failure. The conference failed because of the United States proposal that Manchuria and the former German Pacific Islands now under Japanese mandate be placed under the joint control of four nations."

"After the breakdown of the conference, things transpired rapidly in the United States. The president, as commander in chief, not only devoted himself personally to furthering the propaganda of the Big Navy Building Group but called a special session of Congress and caused it to appropriate one billion dollars for the navy. A five-year program was adopted, under which the United States not only would build sixteen capital ships, eight aircraft carriers, and sixty light cruisers and smaller craft, but would also complete the plans for great defensive fortifications in Guam and the Philippines. It is not necessary for me to declare that the objective of the United States program is to force the submission of our country. Furthermore, I might remark, regarding Japan's attitude to the American program, that ever since the Manchurian emergency, as the financial and economic resources of our country have been drained to meet the expenses of the military, we can no longer find among our countrymen the spirit to build our navy up to the 8-8 program that we laid down in years past."

Manchurian Emergency
"The Manchurian emergency" refers to the September 18, 1931, "Mukden incident," in which local Japanese military commanders staged a fake terrorist bombing against the Japanese-owned South Manchurian Railway as a pretext to invade Manchuria. Months later, Japan created the puppet state of Manchukuo in occupied Manchuria. In 1932, Japan's treachery was exposed in the Lytton Report, resulting in her diplomatic isolation and withdrawal from the League of Nations in 1933.

The 8-8 Program
The "8-8 program" refers to Japanese naval planners' dream to build a balanced battle fleet of eight battleships and eight battlecruisers that they thought sufficient to defend Japan in the 1920s. However, sustaining such an ambitious shipbuilding program would have been extremely taxing on Japanese financial and industrial resources.

"It is clear as day that, as a result of this change, in a few years our navy will fall to a position where it will be only 50 percent, 40 percent, or even 30 percent as strong as that of the United States. It occurred to me that it would be advisable at this time to strike a blow at this nation, which has enjoyed a period of one hundred years of peace, before it can complete the extensive military preparations mentioned above. Furthermore, the United States, being an Anglo-Saxon nation, which traditionally places great store in the matter of security, would never go to war unless she had complete assurance of ultimate victory. Putting it another way, the Americans are a people who can retain their self-respect [in the face of insults] for any number of years, until they can be sure of victory, before they will go to war. For this reason, the United States will not go to war today for ordinary reasons. Because of this, I determined to employ on this occasion extraordinary methods to bring on a war. Accordingly, I unhesitatingly perpetrated the act of violence for which I am being tried. As I am prepared to accept certain death, having violated the laws of our country and having been guilty of using the emperor's battleship for my own purposes, I beg that, by all means, I be sentenced to death under the military penal code. I wish to add one thing in conclusion. If my act of tossing this stone into the waters is successful in bringing on a war, there will be no need to be concerned about the criticism of the world powers, which is naturally to be expected in this case. Even though temporarily we are branded as dishonorable, the historians who record these events in the calmness of peace in the years to come will correctly decide the answer to the question of who really brought on this war."

SECTION 3: MAKI'S VERDICT

"Well, they say that the verdict of the court will be announced today at 3:00 p.m. However, there is nothing about it in the evening papers yet."

"I wonder . . . I believe that the death penalty will be awarded as demanded by the prosecutor."

"Perhaps the sentence will be life imprisonment rather than death, in view of the plea of extenuating circumstances advanced by [the accused's] lawyers."

"No, although under Section 30 of the Naval Penal Law either death or life imprisonment may be awarded, it is prescribed that 'any officer who commences hostilities with a foreign nation without cause shall be punished by death.'"

"What is that book that you are reading?"

"This? Why, it's called 'A Compendium of Laws,' and everything regarding the law is contained in it. According to Section 33 of the Naval Penal Code, 'A person who, without orders, commences hostilities shall be punished by death, life imprisonment or seven or more years' penal servitude.'"

"That being true, I wonder which sentence will be awarded in this case."

"Hmmm, didn't the prosecutor indicate what may be expected? A destroyer commander is a line officer; therefore, Section 30 of the Code should apply."

"But they say that there is now a great deal of propaganda going around in favor of commutation or remission of the sentence."

"That sort of talk is useless. It is the policy of the government to avoid war with the United States no matter what."

"I don't know that they will condemn an officer to death solely to avoid a Japan-United States War."

"Say! There was a story going around when I was a young man about a crown prince named Oroshiya who stabbed a policeman named Tsuda Sanzo to death. Thinking to humor Oroshiya, they requested the death penalty, but fortunately the judge was a fine fellow, who obstinately refused to give in, and thus saved the prince."

Tsuda Sanzo
This tale references the case of Tsuda Sanzo, a deranged Japanese
policeman who attempted to assassinate Russian crown prince Nicholas
(soon to be Tsar Nicholas II) in Otsu, Japan in 1891. Sanzo was sentenced to life imprisonment and died in prison that same year.

In the capital, customers in a barber shop near Hibiya Park jabbered and squabbled while having their hair cut. Suddenly a new customer entered with a newspaper "extra" in one hand. As soon as the other customers saw his reflection in the mirrors, all conversation stopped abruptly.

"Well, it's the death penalty," said the newcomer, as the attention of everyone in the shop was concentrated on him. The reaction of all his listeners was that the sentence was much too severe.

SECTION 4: MAKI'S EXECUTION

Before dawn, a detachment of twenty men, commanded by Lieutenant Wakida, commander of the Guard, emerged from the naval barracks of Yokosuka and proceeded down Uraga Kaido [Street] toward the target range at Otsu. Yokosuka, from Odakicho up to Hirasaka Hill, was still asleep. However, the workmen of the arsenal, who recently had been idle, had arisen at the break of day and climbed the hill with their overcoat collars turned up against the chill of the early morning.

"Say, what's the idea of soldiers being out while it's still dark?"

"Maybe they are on maneuvers . . ."

Thus spoke the uneducated mechanics and workmen as they watched the detachment of the guard with their rifles on their shoulders, swords by their sides, and white puttees on their legs, pass by with eyes rigidly to the front. Gradually the sound of their footsteps died away in the distance. Soon, the marching soldiers were lost to sight. A careful observer, however, would have noticed that the pale face of Lieutenant Wakida, who followed at the rear of the detachment, was flooded with anguish.

The lieutenant was repeating ceaselessly to himself as he walked, "Regardless of what one thinks himself, one must be prepared to fly through fire or water if his orders so direct." How extremely unhappy Lieutenant Wakida must have felt to have to give the order to shoot to death his classmate and closest friend.

Lieutenant Wakida's detachment was on its way to execute the death sentence imposed upon Lieutenant Eitaro Maki of the Imperial Navy, found guilty of the grave crime of sinking a United States battleship. Just about the time that day began to break over Boso Peninsula, the detachment reached a broad parade ground close to the beach at Otsu. Near the center of the parade ground, where the target range was located, the pale morning mist still obscured the scene.

When the detachment arrived, Lieutenant Wakida reported to the chief of staff, who had preceded them to this spot. Then Wakida heard the chief of staff's voice saying, "The commander in chief has also arrived. He is, as you know, a close friend of Lieutenant Maki's father."

This was the first execution of a death penalty in the navy since Warrant Officer Sankichi Furita faced a firing squad after a murder conviction two hundred years ago. Due to the importance of this affair, many high-ranking officers had come to Yokosuka from the Navy Department in Tokyo to witness the execution. The target range was crowded with officers from the Navy Club who had taken up positions with the vice minister of the navy, the chief of the Naval Affairs Bureau, the judge advocate general of the navy, the vice chief of the naval general staff, and many other chiefs of departments in the front ranks. A large crowd of civilians from Otsu entered the parade ground uninvited and were watching the proceedings with the closest attention. Military police and civil police, muttering and bickering among themselves, packed the crowd in ten- and twenty-deep.

"Pretty soon they will kill him, eh?"

"Isn't there any way of saving him?"

"If you save him, it would mean that the United States would declare war."

"He killed 400 Americans by himself so there's no help for him."

"The detachment will shoot over there—Oh!"

"They will, of course, fire only one volley, will they not?"

A black navy automobile, with the convertible roof down, sped into the enclosure. It had been sent from the navy prison in Otsu. The prisoner to be executed today was carried in the car. The crowd, with lowered heads, avoided looking at the prisoner. Ten minutes later, tall Lieutenant Maki appeared and strode with long steps to a dike in the rear of the target range. Then, waving aside the bleached cotton mask brought up by one of the guards, he took his stand without affectation while the semblance of an artless smile brightened his face. Ten paces away, the detachment, commanded by Lieutenant Wakida, arranged in two ranks of six men each, stood facing the prisoner.

Swish! went Lieutenant Wakida's sword as he drew it from the scabbard. Just now, when it seemed that the morning sun was on the point of breaking through the clouds and flooding the scene with bright sunlight, Lieutenant Wakida's harsh voice softly rang out and was echoed by the ranks.

"With three ball cartridges—load!"

The magazines of twelve rifles clicked and the next command was awaited.

"Standing load! Aim!"

The eyes of the hundred-or-so spectators turned by one accord to the face of the prisoner. But the prisoner's face was immobile and did not indicate by so much as a wink of the eye that he had heard the command. As all awaited the next command, the order burst from the mouth of the detachment commander: "Fire!"

Lieutenant Maki's firing squad at Yokosuka. Illustration by Katsuichi Kabashima in *Nichibei-sen Miraiki. University of Maryland Prange collection*

Japanese War Fantasy

With a roar, the rifles spoke. As the noise rang in their ears, the spectators were torn between the desires to look and not to look. Many of the people involuntarily closed their eyes. Finally, the crowd opened their eyes and looked at the spot ten paces away expecting to see the fallen body of Lieutenant Maki. How could this be? There stood Lieutenant Maki, his tall body proudly erect with the morning breeze gently fluttering his clothing.

"How did that happen?"

They could not believe their eyes. Rubbing their eyes, the crowd again stared at the spot. However, rub their eyes as they might, they could not erase the sight of the prisoner still standing straight and looking calmly into their faces. At this moment, the shrill voice of the detachment commander again rang out.

"Aim! Fire!!!"

The second time, there were none in the crowd who closed their eyes as the bullets sped eastward. The shots raised a yellow dust cloud on the dike. The target, however, did not fall. He continued to stand erect as before.

"Commander! Here, commander," called the chief of staff, starting to run toward the detachment commander. However, at this moment Lieutenant Wakida called out the order for the third shot.

"Aim! Fire!"

The spectators looked for the third time. As one, they exclaimed, "Look at the prisoner. He is still alive and standing, motionless, bathed in the dazzling sunlight!" The commander in chief, the vice minister of the navy, the vice chief of the general staff, and the prison warden were struck speechless and did not know what to say. Only the chief of staff found his voice, and he roared, "What are you doing?? What's the meaning of this?!?"

"I don't know," answered the detachment commander. "It certainly is mystifying."

"At any rate, fire once more."

"I am sorry, but the cartridges are . . . ." began the detachment commander.

At this moment, the commander in chief opened his mouth to speak for the first time. "No! Chief of staff, do not fire more than three times," he said in a voice that silenced them all.

The witnesses then immediately began to discuss how the matter had happened.

"I can't understand it. Not one of the bullets from twelve rifles, all aimed at him, struck him!"

"And they tried three times, too," said a person who heard this remark and was completely mystified. "If the rifles had been empty, I would understand, but . . ."

"No, absolutely they were loaded. Didn't the shots strike the bank and raise a dust cloud?"

"It was a miracle, wasn't it?"

"Perhaps. There is an old tale about the official of the ancient Hojo government who thought to cut down a Nichiren priest, but his sword only cut through air. Possibly this is similar to that occurrence."

"Indeed, in this world we can see supernatural things sometimes."

The suspicious chief of staff was sternly interrogating Lieutenant Wakida, the detachment commander, and [Wakida's former] classmate, Lieutenant Maki, the prisoner. However, this single-minded official had no definite plan in mind and conducted his investigation in a desultory fashion. In short, except for inquiring of the soldiers as to where they had aimed, he did not seem to be able to think up any other questions. In reply, the men answered that "it seemed as if a light shown from the face of Lieutenant Maki," and, beyond this, they could add nothing further to solve the mystery.

The officers at the Navy Club, in talking about the esteemed Lieutenant Maki, said that, in truth, there had been no mistake about the fact that a light seemed to shine from his face when the soldiers had aimed at it. Even though there were some who did not believe this, they felt apologetic and concealed the fact to the best of their ability. There were some of the soldiers, however, who, upon being questioned about the matter, answered, "Because so many rifles were there to fire at the lieutenant, I thought that it would not matter if I, alone, turned my aim slightly away from the prisoner when I fired." If all twelve soldiers had harbored the same idea, even though they had fired one hundred times instead of three, the results would have been the same, and it would have been impossible to have taken the life of the lieutenant.

This story is fiction, of course, but is it not possible that I have correctly interpreted what would really happen were this the truth? Without a doubt, people who believe in mystic occurrences might even see in an actual case of this kind something of the mysterious.

SECTION 5: THE BLACK KITE

Under the military penal code, which covers both the army and the navy, it is the unwritten law that if a prisoner escapes death after being fired at three times by the execution squad, he must be released and set free. It is not entirely clear why the authorities did not want to apply this law to Lieutenant Maki's case, for there does not appear to have been any special reason for not so doing. At any rate, Lieutenant Maki was finally released from custody under this law, albeit with a perceptible unwillingness on the part of the authorities. However, he received an administrative order releasing him only twelve minutes before he was completely divested of all military rank and decorations.

The government was thrown into consternation by the unexpected outcome of the case. No matter what explanations were offered, the cold fact remained that a foreign commander and his flagship had been destroyed, and the culprit who had perpetrated the crime remained alive. If this had been done by a small country, such as Costa Rica or Panama, the great United States would have struck as swiftly as shooting a pigeon on the wing. It was apparent, therefore, that the release of Lieutenant Maki must revive the unreasonably harsh demands of the United States.

However, public opinion at this time did not demand that the lieutenant, who had escaped death through application of the unwritten law of the military penal code, be again brought before a firing squad. The reason for this was widely published news in Japan's newspapers: the day that Lieutenant Maki was released, about ten Japanese were lynched by a San Francisco mob in reprisal for the lieutenant's escape from death.

In both Japan and America, the situation developed rapidly. In Japan, public endorsement of the actions of Lieutenant Maki increased with extreme rapidity, while, in America, people everywhere, in the cities, in the country, in the mountains, all urged the US government to bring Japan to answer for the incident. Furthermore, the calling of a special session of the cabinet in Japan and, in the United States, the change of the secretaries of state, war and navy and the chief of naval operations to the War Party were acts that failed, to say the least, to calm public opinion. Thus, everything turned out exactly as Lieutenant Maki had wished it. Japan, which had started this affair, quickly roused itself and took action. A new cabinet was installed that immediately ordered the expulsion of the United States ambassador from Japan. Five days after the installation of the new cabinet, a declaration of war on the United States was promulgated by imperial rescript.

"It has finally come," said a naked old man reading the newspaper extra telling of the declaration of war to a group of about fifty people in the public bathhouse and then spiritedly plunging into the pool. The bather splashed around in the tub with much noise. Some of them complained that the starting of war would undoubtedly raise the prices of commodities, and some were pessimistic and warned that Japan would be seriously embarrassed through its inability to sell its silk. However, the great majority of the patrons of the bathhouse were saying, "There is nothing to be excited about or to make a fuss over just because the inevitable has happened." They remained calm and undisturbed. The bathers did raise questions regarding Japan's strategy and diplomacy in the war . . .

"The important question is, what will Great Britain, Russia, and China do? I think that Great Britain will remain neutral for a while. She has no time to bother with affairs in the Pacific, things being as unsettled as they are in Europe . . ."

"Hasn't Russia been very quiet recently, also?"

"Russia? Oh, since year before last, our army has been prepared for war, and Russia knows it. They also know that if they make a move, they will lose the maritime provinces."

"All right, what about China?"

"China? China, of course, will be an enemy," said a neighbor whose face was as red as a boiled lobster and covered with steam from the bath. "This being as clear as day to all concerned, the Japanese army's principal business will be to seize the 400-odd provinces of that country."

"Don't you think that the American airplanes will attack Kyushu from a base in China?"

"If that should appear likely to happen, the Japanese army will exert its entire energy to wiping out such bases."

"That's all right, but they say that this war will be a naval war, pure and simple. If the navy wins, it will not need any help from the army. On the other hand, if it is defeated, no matter how firmly the army holds out, it will avail nothing."

"To change the subject for a moment, may I inquire where your younger brother went after he failed his conscription examination for service with the colors?"

"He went straight to the Philippines, then Gum, they tell me."

Vought O3U-1 Corsair reconnaissance aircraft from USS *Augusta* (CA-31) on a barge in Subic Bay, Philippines. In the distance at left, submarines sit alongside tender USS *Canopus* (AS-9) and destroyers flank tender USS *Black Hawk* (AD-9). *Naval Historical Center (NH 51872)*

"It's not pronounced 'Gum,' but Guam. It's an American island lying due south of our island of Saipan in the southern archipelago. They must also occupy Guam quickly and at once."

"Having carried out these steps, the plan then is to seize America next, I suppose?"

"No. It's not so simple as that because, midway to the States, there are the Hawaiian Islands."

"I have heard a lot of good things about Hawaii. They tell me that the Japanese who have emigrated to Hawaii raise bananas, pineapple, and sugar, and far outnumber the peoples of all other races and countries in those islands."

"They can help us a lot. However, it is our country's duty to stir up and incite the Japanese in Hawaii to attack the Americans there from within the islands."

Japanese immigrants arriving in Honolulu, ca. 1910. *Library of Congress (LC 10-3129-18)*

"Don't count your chickens before they hatch. No matter how much those Japanese in Hawaii make a fuss, they can't do much because they haven't any arms."

"Arms! Excuse me, but what did *Shiko Edo* and others say? 'If you do not have any weapons, advance with bamboo spears!' Please observe this rule also. In the hour of need, pierce your enemy's stomach with a bamboo spear. Try to emulate the skillfulness of the black kite, for it is a lucky omen."

Shiko Edo
"Shiko Edo" apparently refers to *bushido* values. During Japan's Edo period, 1603–1868, the term *shiko* was far more common than the term *bushido*.

"Unfortunately, bamboo does not grow on those islands," said someone. "Now, if it were sugar cane, why, any amount of that grows there."

"There are bamboo spears there, all right," said a discerning hearer, "But they might just as well be bare-handed when they meet an enemy equipped with machine guns, airplanes, army tanks and poison gas apparatus. This war is going to be a mechanical and scientific war, I tell you."

Perhaps most of these statements were based on things they had read in newspapers and magazines, but they must not be entirely dismissed. It was a godsend that, for the last five or six years, army and navy propaganda, spread by word of mouth, by the written word, and through expositions, had planted the military spirit everywhere throughout the nation.

CHAPTER 2
The Deserter

SECTION 1: KAWANO'S MOTHER

The scene of the story now shifts back to the little radio shop of Mister Yamano in Tokiwacho, in the city of Dairen, Manchuria. As Chieko, the wife, entered the sitting room with her husband, she asked, "Did you hear the news just now? They say that an American warship has been sunk."

"No, I was repairing a radio set at a customer's house, and I did not hear it."

"I heard it just now over the shop set," said Chieko, suddenly raising her voice. "The commander who sank the American ship is our lieutenant named Maki. Of all people!"

"The ship was the *Nara*, too," she continued as she drew near to Yamano, watching him closely.

"When I heard the news, my heart involuntarily beat so very fast that I was afraid that my customer noticed it."

"Anyway, he [Lieutenant Maki] certainly is a rash officer. It is a coincidence that Lieutenant Maki, whom you know so well, should be the one to do this."

"No! No!" Chieko cried, "I personally do not understand this affair, but you remember that after your dear mother died, you deserted from the navy and hid your identity here. The real cause of your desertion was the unsympathetic and cruel behavior of that very officer, was it not?"

Looking at it from that point of view, Chieko's statement was correct. Yamano let the matter drop. He was deeply regretful of the actions that had culminated in his desertion. It occurred in the spring of last year when, as

Seaman First Class Tsuyoshi Kawano, he had arrived at Yokosuka aboard the destroyer *Nara*. Receiving the news that his aged mother, whom he held dearer than heaven or earth, lay sick in a miserable hovel at Oimachi, near Tokyo, he hastened to the capital as soon as he was granted shore leave, which luckily occurred on the fourth day in port.

On his arrival at the hovel, near which some children were playing store, he noticed that the front door of the house was shut. Entering, he saw his mother in a small, three-mat room, groaning and holding her stomach. Alarmed over her condition, the sailor, without thought of the expense, hastily took his mother to the naval charity hospital in Tsukiji, Tokyo, for consultation with a medical officer.

"Cancer, I think," gravely announced the medical officer after an examination. "If this is the case, we must operate. How old is she?"

"Exactly fifty years old."

"My, she is still very young! I think that she will come out all right in that case," said the doctor. "Ask for special shore leave and come to the hospital tomorrow morning at ten o'clock. At that time, I will give her a blood transfusion."

After the operation the next day, the sailor submitted himself for the blood transfusion to his mother, after which he returned late at night to his ship. He determined to return to the hospital at daybreak the next morning.

"May I have permission to speak to her?" asked the sailor before he departed from the hospital. Approaching his mother, he whispered in her ear, "I am going to get special permission to return here tomorrow. Tonight, I must return to Yokosuka, but tomorrow evening I will come back here as early as possible."

His mother nodded sadly. The sailor then took his leave and boarded the streetcar, but the sad face of his mother haunted him continuously.

"It's too bad that I can't stay with Mother," he reproached himself as he rode on the owl car. This sailor, who sent his mother the greater part of his monthly pay of 16 yen (which he received as a first-class seaman), could not, of course, be expected to make many trips to Tokyo. However, the pitiful condition of his mother outweighed any other considerations now. His grief and contrition were especially poignant because he had become so wrapped up in his affair with Chieko that he had forgotten his mother.

Owl Cars
An "owl car" was a streetcar that ran all night long.

However, even the love of Chieko in that Yokosuka lodging house was powerless now to make this loyal son forget the sad condition of his mother even for a moment.

That night, he lay awake in his narrow bed on the destroyer, awaiting the return of his officer. The next day, after hearing the full story of Seaman First Class Kawano, the officer replied, "I think you are lying when you say that your mother is dangerously ill. In the first place, according to your records you have no mother named Chise Yamamura. Probably, this 'Yamamura' is really 'Umemura' [a village] and 'Chise' is 'Chie' [the given name of his sweetheart]. Yes, I think that's it . . . It's mighty convenient to have a nice nineteen-year-old 'mother' for a relative!"

"No, section chief, you are mistaken," vigorously objected Kawano, wondering which back-stabbing sailor had fed the section officer this disinformation. "What I have told you is the truth. My mother comes from the Kawano family. Please speak to the captain about this request of mine."

Undeterred by the section chief's obvious lack of desire to speak to the captain about the matter, Kawano hopefully awaited the ship commander's decision, because the latter was known to be kindhearted.

"The destroyer is to leave port at once," announced the section officer upon his return from the captain's quarters. "Furthermore, the captain said that because there is nothing in your papers to indicate that you have a mother, your request to leave your duties is denied."

There was no help for the difficult situation in which the sailor found himself. Last night, in the stiff wind, some fishing boats had been wrecked in the offing near Nii Island off Izu. Emergency orders had been received from the naval station for the destroyer squadron, headed by *Nara*, to proceed at once to assist the wrecked fishermen.

Next day, upon return from the rescue expedition, Seaman First Class Kawano received a terse telegram: "Chise Yamamura failed to make satisfactory progress and died at five o'clock."

Japanese sailors in formation at stern of destroyer, 1927. *Library of Congress (LC-B2-4301-17)*

At the time of the funeral, few sailors were allowed shore leave, and Kawano was not one of them. This saddened him very much. After the funeral, Kawano went to thank the kind doctors of the charity hospital. While there, a nurse informed him that his mother died because one blood transfusion was insufficient. She said that they had waited for his return to make another transfusion, but his failure to return was fatal. After hearing this, Tsuyoshi Kawano vanished.

SECTION 2: THE GOOD LIFE IN MANCHURIA

"Niiya, come back when you have closed up the shop."

When the Manchurian shop boy returned, Chieko, the wife, went inside the house and went to bed. Although it was spring, it was still cold in

Manchuria. Snow beat against the glass of the windows. "I wonder what we should do about this matter?" inquired Chieko anxiously. "Now that this has happened, what will you do?" Her husband remained silent. The wife, who knew her husband was a man who would remain silent on a subject until he decided to talk, quickly changed the subject. "Today, I heard at the neighbor's that Dairen is going to present four patriotic airplanes to the navy. They want each household to subscribe two yen toward the cost of these planes. Shall we subscribe?"

Husband Tsuyoshi remained as silent as a stone, showing no interest in the airplane fundraising.

"Why don't you answer?!" exclaimed the young wife, sobbing, "I came way over here for you, and I have only you to depend on."

Tsuyoshi finally broke his silence. "I am a wicked man. In truth, I brought you here from far away . . . I suppose that you would like to return now and then to Yokosuka to see your mother. Letters alone do not suffice to relieve concern in such cases."

"Don't say such things. You know that it makes no difference to me—Manchuria or Siberia—anywhere that you go, I will go with you."

"But no matter where I go, I can't use my real name. I am like a robber cat, always hiding myself, and it is very distasteful to me. Even today when I went to repair the radio in the middle school dormitory, the officers on duty at the school said, 'Radio man, you have a very fine physique. Have you been conscripted yet? What is your regimental district?' I became very disconcerted."

"But Manchuria is, of course, a carefree place. Think back to the time you were in Japan. Didn't you have to flee even though you had the large city of Tokyo to hide in?"

"After mother's funeral, at the time I deserted, I went to a friend's house in Shinagawa, threw away my uniform, and then fled by train to Osaka."

"What did you expect to do in Osaka?"

"I did not have any particular plan in mind. My only idea was that Tokyo and Yokosuka were dangerous places for me to be," answered the man, shaking violently as he recalled that terrible time. "Then, at the ticket window of the Umeda Station, when one of the station officials called to me—'Hey, wait a moment, you!'—I figuratively died a hundred deaths."

"What did he want?" asked the wife, lowering her voice.

"Oh, it was only that I had been confused and had forgotten to show him my ticket!"

He doubled up with laughter as he spoke. He now had a social position in Dairen, but he remembered the time when he had thought to return a second time to Tokyo from Osaka but was deterred therefrom by the fear that he would be forced to drift here and there like a homeless dog in the city, fearing to even visit the homes of his relatives.

"The knowledge of electricity that I had acquired in the navy helped me in my difficulty, and I succeeded in establishing myself here in my present position as a radio man. However, although my work provides me with food, at times I feel much worse than the lowest beggar."

"Just before I deserted, when I was in Yokosuka, a man whom I did not know came up to my house saying, 'This is a message from Mr. Kawano of Dairen,' and handed me a letter in which was enclosed a money order. I felt at the time as if I had been bewitched by a fox," said the man. Suddenly growing serious as he continued, "After that, I deserted, but it was not entirely my fault alone. I was afraid of court martial and imprisonment, it is true, but it was really the circumstances surrounding the death of my mother that culminated in my desertion and made me dislike the navy."

"That is what Lieutenant Maki did to you?"

"I have been obsessed with that idea until the recent declaration of war," he answered. "However, since that has occurred, my bitter feeling and resentment against both the navy and Lieutenant Maki has vanished."

"What do you think you will do?" asked Chieko, returning to her original query. "Do you feel like giving yourself up?"

"I don't know what to do. It's troubling me greatly. Today, the incident with the officers at the middle school touched a nerve. Yet I can't go on being a businessman under the circumstances."

Chieko did not answer, and her husband continued. "Say, this war is going to be a serious matter for Japan. It is going to decide whether Japan, which has existed for 3,000 years, will be destroyed or will flourish more than ever. On whose shoulders will the responsibility for the outcome of the war rest? Just at first, surely not on the Japanese people, nor on the government, nor on the army. No. The responsibility will rest entirely on us sailors of the Imperial Navy."

Chieko nodded, and the man broached the subject of his future plans.

"Come what may, I must surrender myself. Perhaps they will defer my imprisonment and let me serve with the navy. But what about you?"

"Oh, I will go back to my home village, as you suggested. However, no matter what happens, I will always be Mrs. Chieko Kawano."

As the husband was on the point of speaking, his young wife, shame-facedly referring to something wicked, said, "If you do as you say, don't worry about me. I will be able to do something or the other . . ."

SECTION 3: TOKAIDO EXPRESS CHATTER

The Tokaido Express was crowded with sailors in wrinkled uniforms, the pendants of whose caps bore the words "Yokosuka Naval Barracks." Some of the caps had fallen off and exposed the long uncut hair of their wearers. Furthermore, it was apparent to everyone who noted their beards and the insignia of rank on their sleeves that these sailors were not men of the active list of the navy.

"Well, you have finally been called out for naval service?" inquired one of the passengers to his neighbor in a voice of admiration.

"Yes, because of the big war. I guess that we may be assigned to some kind of active service involving duty similar to that on a minelayer or on a minesweeper. You see, we were called up for service on trawlers."

"What do they use trawlers for?"

"Either as substitutes for minesweepers or as exterminators of submarines."

"Will the enemy's submarines come way over to Japan?"

"I don't know whether they will come or not. However, as the American submarine cruisers can cruise 25,000 sea miles on one load of fuel oil, we can't be careless."

"Indeed," said the passenger admiringly. "However, I did not realize that it was exactly 25,000 sea miles from America to Japan."

"Don't joke about it! There is a saying that in making the trip from America to Japan, travelers become so tired that they are afflicted with a disease resembling paralysis after traveling 4,500 sea miles. Calling this roughly 5,000 miles, that means that in two round trips there are 20,000 miles."

"If they get sick after a single one-way trip, I don't think they would want to make any more trips . . ."

"America has a base with submarines closer than you think. A small submarine flotilla is stationed at Manila, in the Philippines, which is only 1,714 sea miles from Yokosuka."

US Navy Porpoise-class submarines in Manila, 1939 (*left to right*): USS *Pike* (SS-173), USS *Tarpon* (SS-175), USS *Porpoise* (SS-172), USS *Perch* (SS-176), and USS *Permit* (SS-178). *Naval Historical Center (NH 99672)*

"It's rather peculiar, this threat of submarines coming from America, and the fact that American submarines are stationed at Manila."

When the train arrived at Ofuna, the sailors transferred to the electric cars of the Yokosuka Line. The number of sailors was enormous. Crowded in the coaches in uncountable numbers were numerous sailors who seemed to be of the same year's class. They jammed all the entrances and exits and were noisily calling.

Ofuna
Ofuna was an Imperial Japanese Navy installation located in Kamakura, near Yokohama. From 1942 to 1945, Ofuna hosted a prisoner-of-war camp for high-value American submariners and pilots including Louis Zamperini and Pappy Boyington.

"Say, are you still alive?!?"

"What? Who is this fellow cultivating a mustache? I wonder, what's the idea . . . Is he a time-expired man?"

"How do I know? It's probably the conductor."

"Do you mean 'conducter' or 'conductor?'" Be careful of your pronunciation. You are a military man now, you know."

"I meant 'conductor,' of course!"

"Well, he is not the conductor, for conductors have no use for mustaches."

"Then he is probably the chauffeur of the patrol of the penitentiary. Patrol chauffeurs are always extremely dignified men, you know."

When the train arrived at Yokosuka, these several hundred sailors in wrinkled and soiled uniforms streamed out of the black station. The broad street of Kusugauracho, which ran in front of the station and seemed to end in the harbor, was packed with old timers moving about and visiting with each other.

At the naval barracks on Kusugauracho Street, tents had been pitched in the space from the front gate to the first barracks. Several dozen mobilization officials were waiting there on the alert. In the largest tent, the chief of personnel of the naval station, looking like Togashi Saemon guarding the barrier at Adaka, sat waiting at his desk, puffing on a cigarette.

Togashi Saemon
Togashi Saemon was the protagonist in the popular kabuki drama *Kanjincho*, in which Togashi is the guardian of a checkpoint that is screening travelers in search of a disguised enemy infiltrator.

"Count off by fours," called the corporal of the guard from time to time as he straightened out the ranks of the conscripts.

Each of the old timers, who had been formed into four groups, would raise his hand and salute, at the same time calling out his name as he came up to the barrier.

"Taro Monmaki!"

The mobilization sergeant, who was standing by the side of the mobilization officer, appeared to be checking off the names from an alphabetical roster. As each name was called, he would raise his voice and yell, "All right. Next!"

"Kenzo Onotera."

"All right. Next!"

These old timers had hastened to the aid of the country in its time of emergency from all corners of the empire. There were men here from all the prefectures, from Mie in the west to Hokkaido and Sakhalin Island in the north."

The medical officers from the neighboring naval hospital were present to assist in the mobilization. From the chief surgeon down, they busied themselves conducting the physical examinations of the newly mobilized men.

This activity had been underway for three days when a sailor, youthful-looking among the old timers, in reply to the mobilization noncommissioned officer's "Next!" stepped forward one pace and called, "Tsuyoshi Kawano!"

"Kawano," repeated the NCO, searching through his roster of names, "Why, that name is not on this list," he continued, raising his eyes and glaring suspiciously at the sailor in front of him. "Say, this sailor's cap pendant is not correct."

Instead of "Yokosuka Naval Barracks," the band around the sailor's cap bore the words "15th Destroyer Flotilla, Imperial Japanese Navy."

"What is this, you?" inquired the NCO. "Are you a member of the First Reserve?"

"No, I am on active service," nervously answered the sailor. "I am Seaman First Class Tsuyoshi Kawano, who deserted exactly one year ago from the destroyer *Nara* of the 15th Destroyer Flotilla."

"So, you are a deserter," said the NCO, opening his eyes widely. "Why did you do it?"

"Please let me go with the others on the ships."

SECTION 4: STRATEGIC THINKING

In a restaurant on the fifth floor of a newspaper plant near Sukiyabashi, in Tokyo, a group of five or six newspaper men were gathered in a corner drinking coffee and talking in low voices.

"Has any news come in?"

"The London telegrams have just arrived," said one of the group, producing a piece of paper and showing it to the others.

USS *Utah* in the late 1920s. *Naval Historical Center (NH 50227)*

"The American training ship *Wyoming* and the target ship *Utah* are being converted into battleships in the navy yards at New York and Mare Island by workmen working day and night."

USS *Wyoming*
USS *Wyoming* (BB-32) was the lead ship of her class of dreadnought battleships when launched in 1910, patrolled the North Sea during World War I, and was converted into a training ship after the 1930 London Naval Treaty. During World War II, *Wyoming* operated in the Chesapeake Bay and trained 35,000 gunners for the wartime navy.

USS *Wyoming* (BB-32) in drydock in New York,
ca. 1931. *Naval Historical Center (NH 59961)*

USS *Wyoming* sailors bustle on deck
while another capital ship trails in the
distance. *Naval Historical Center (NH
76549)*

USS *Wyoming* crew portrait, ca. 1932. *Naval Historical Center (NH 83693)*

USS *Wyoming* underway, 12-inch guns trained starboard, March 1930. *Wyoming* was converted to a training ship after the 1930 London Naval Treaty. *Naval Historical Center (NARA 80-G-466464)*

Japanese War Fantasy

"What are these training and target ships anyway?" asked one of the group as he finished reading the dispatch.

"These were ships that were decommissioned as a result of the London conference. Under the agreement made at that conference, they were to be stripped of their guns, boilers, and armor, after which they could be used as training ships or for some similar purpose."

"The Japanese ship *Hiei* is also one of these training ships," said someone.

Japanese battle cruiser *Hiei*, converted to a training ship, August 1933. *Naval Historical Center (NH 89175)*

Battleship *Hiei*
IJN battleship *Hiei* patrolled the Chinese coast during World War I, was converted to a gunnery training ship in 1929 under the terms of the Washington Naval Conference, was modernized in 1937, and in 1941 escorted the aircraft carriers that attacked Pearl Harbor. *Hiei* was sunk during the naval battles of Guadalcanal in November 1942.

"If that is true, fellow, it will increase their capital ships from fifteen to seventeen. That is very disquieting."

"Yes. That four-billion-dollar building program is still only in the blue-print stage, so they have to exert themselves to quickly repair their old ships," said one of the reporters who frequently visited the navy department, putting the palm of his left hand over his mouth as he spoke. "So, it is all right for Japan to do likewise, as we are doing with the *Hiei*."

"Even so, we will have only ten capital ships, as compared to their seventeen. Is that safe?"

"I can't exactly say. However, generally the so-called capital ship is one on which there are guns [of ordinary caliber] as well as those of very large caliber. Now, if we compare the large-caliber guns . . . ," said the navy reporter, bringing out his notebook, "the United States have 182 heavy guns while we have ninety-six."

"Oh, that is terrifying. Is that the truth?"

"Sure, it's true. I just got that information from the navy department's propaganda bureau."

"If that is so, it is certainly hard to swallow. Can we win with only ninety-six guns?"

"Oh, it's all right. I'll guarantee that," said a brave member of the group. "Why do you ask? The outcome will depend on naval strategy. The attacker must use a very large force, but, as Japan's plan is to defend the Western Pacific, she will not need a very large force."

"Ho! You know how to brag, don't you? Who was your teacher? Was it Masanori Ito or Shinsaku Hirata?"

Masanori Ito and Shinsaku Hirata
Masanori Ito (1889–1962) was a prominent journalist who knew many top Japanese naval commanders and who authored the book *The End of the Imperial Japanese Navy* in 1956. Shinsaku Hirata (1899–1936) was a popular militarist-nationalist writer who promoted anti-Western ideology and predicted that a Pacific war would begin with a Japanese attack on Pearl Harbor in a widely publicized 1933 book.

"Please listen quietly," said one of the group who was a student of the white man's military strategy. "In all the history of war, there is not a case in which an expeditionary force was successful. Napoleon was destroyed at Moscow. The Baltic Fleet was destroyed in the Sea of Japan. And yet the Baltic fleet seemed very powerful."

"No. I don't agree with you," contradicted the navy reporter who had first spoken. "It's the same thing as saying that because Lieutenant Shirase's South Pole expedition was a failure, Admiral [Richard E.] Byrd's expedition would also have to have been a failure."

"Well, I also saw the pictures of that South Pole expedition, and it appeared to me that, had he been as careful about his preparations for the expedition, he may have been as successful as Admiral Byrd."

"It is reasonable to assume that the brains of the American navy hold similar ideas to those of Admiral Byrd. Don't you think that, if they intend to fight a strong power in the Far East, they have paved the way by consolidating a position in China?"

"No, you are mistaken. It was because their preparations in China are not fully developed yet that Lieutenant Maki decided to make his attack to bring on the war right now."

"That's so. You argue well. China is a secondary matter—a place for the use of auxiliary ships. As far as capital ships are concerned, Japan's preparation is based on strategy involving the ratio of three to five. For that reason, the question that now faces us is not that of capital ships."

"Is that so?"

"That's an empty argument. As Mr. Hirotoku Mizuno says in his [book] *This War*, in the Russo-Japanese War, Admiral Togo's fleet was armed with fifty-eight 8-inch-or-greater caliber guns while [Admiral Zinovy] Rozhestvensky's fleet, which came to attack it, was armed with only fifty guns. Wasn't it because of the fact that the attacking fleet did not have more guns than the defending fleet that Rozhestvensky's fleet was defeated?"

Admiral Heihachiro Togo, hero of the Russo-Japanese War. *Library of Congress (LC-H25-20249-C)*

"He was very foolish. It is necessary always that the attacking force be 50 percent superior to the defending," the self-styled strategist said.

"Listen to him. He is giving the Shirase model of Rozhestvensky's strategy. But, in the present case, the position of the American navy is very much different from that. They have 182 heavy guns as compared to our mere ninety-six. Your argument is defective, is it not?"

"If we depend on our strategy in the Russo-Japanese War, it will be dangerous. This was different," said the cautious one who sat across the table.

"I think, if I were to say the truth, that both our navy and our country will experience a much more terrible war this time than was the case at the time of the Russo-Japanese War. It is not only a matter of the number of ships and guns; there are other things also. The American naval expeditionary force will not be modeled after that of the Baltic Fleet in the Russo-Japanese War. That fleet of sixteen ships cruised around the world in 1905, but, since that time, thirty years have passed, during which the American navy has conducted intensive research into the strategy of a Far Eastern War."

"I say that is foolish," protested the courageous strategist. "My idea is that the strength of a navy does not depend entirely upon the capital ship. The cruiser, the destroyer, and the submarine are also important. The expert chess player manipulating his lesser pieces defeats his opponent. In naval warfare, like in chess, the skill with which the auxiliaries are used is also most important. Luckily, Japan excels over America in auxiliary vessels, does she not?"

"No, she certainly does not. It is only in capital ships that our navy does not feel a shortage."

SECTION 5: NAVAL PERSONNEL

America had rebuilt as battleships *Wyoming* (26,000 tons) and *Utah* (22,000 tons) to their original, pretreaty specifications, while Japan had similarly completed *Hiei* (26,300 tons). Furthermore, both nations had converted certain powerful ships by means of adding flying decks, thus turning them into regular aircraft carriers. Of course, it was not clear exactly what ships were so converted. However, as both countries employ a great number of spies in the enemy's shipyards, it is probable that the governments knew the names of such ships.

In addition, both countries began the construction of a large number of destroyers and submarines after the beginning of the war. Also, besides requisitioning trawlers for coast-defense purposes, they began to build a new type of ship called the cruiser-submarine.

To provide personnel for these new ships when they would be commissioned, the American navy exerted every effort to meet the situation. As was to be expected, the problem of recruiting stymied American naval authorities, even though they exerted themselves to the utmost. This was the case even in the face of the great financial and economic strength of the United States.

"Navy needs you" poster with art by James Montgomery Flagg, ca. 1917. *Library of Congress (LC CPH 3g10238)*

Posters were displayed everywhere, on street corners, in saloons, railroad stations, theaters, and art galleries. George Washington was shown on these posters, with his finger pointing at the observer, while underneath was written the words "America Wants Your Help." Other pictures showed the actress Clara Bow kissing a sailor's white hat. Every day, in the cities, parades were held in which the navy band, playing some stirring march of the late bandleader [John Philip] Sousa, led a march followed by troops carrying banners proclaiming, "The United States Navy Needs You."

Clara Bow, American movie starlet in the late 1920s and early 1930s. *Library of Congress (LC-B2-6486-3)*

Young people who did not understand anything about national policy laughed out loud when they saw the navy's desperate recruiting efforts.

"Why should we risk our lives against unknown Japanese? It is distasteful to us to think of crossing the Pacific for such a purpose. For whose sake is this war being fought? It is to return Manchuria to the Chi-Chi-Chinamen."

Even despite this, to say that the American navy failed completely to achieve success in its emergency navy mobilization program would not be true. There were some who did not object, and more than 200,000 applicants were received throughout the entire country. This number exceeded the mobilization quota five times. As a result of assigning these hastily trained recruits to the fleet, the effect was the same as would be expected if woodcutters from the mountains were taken and sent to sea as fishermen. Furthermore, although efforts were made to assign the new recruits only to the expeditionary fleet, the new manpower was also put aboard capital ships and new cruisers, where it was found that they were good for nothing except to consume the food stores and deplete the supply rooms. In other words, they were decidedly encumbrances.

US sailors man a 5-inch/51-caliber gun on USS *Black Hawk* (AD-9), ca. 1937. *Naval Historical Center (NH 101147)*

"As the number of deserters from the ships of the American navy has become very large, all shore leave for personnel has been terminated," stated a dispatch received in Japan from Mexico. Although it is not known how much dependence could be placed in that dispatch, it is not thought that it was a complete falsehood.

Considering conditions in America, we are prone to think that Japan was very fortunate. However, although twenty to thirty new ships had been launched, the needs of Japan's navy were not satisfied. Hundreds of former servicemen had to dig into the bottom of their chests and fish out their wrinkled old uniforms.

In a time of need such as the present, scores of people felt that it was wrong for the navy department to deny a splendid man such as Lieutenant Maki the opportunity to resume his destroyer command. Thus, the navy personnel department issued an order to reinstate Maki:

Appointed Naval Lieutenant: Eitaro Maki

To command destroyer *Kurumi*: Navy Lieutenant Eitaro Maki

This order acknowledged the changing times in Japan. Accordingly, the morning following the order's issuance, Lieutenant Maki appeared at the naval barracks in Yokosuka. Shaking hands with the chief of the supply section, he made arrangements to inspect the provisions that had been made for the crew on the newly built destroyer *Kurumi*.

"I request only that the chief of the torpedo section be a man of the first-line service. This is because this ship is armed with torpedoes of the very newest design," said Maki. The new commander flipped through the roster of the crew for this newest-model destroyer.

"Everybody is saying that it would be a good thing if this ship were not equipped with torpedoes that shoot straight," laughingly replied his brother officer. "That's because you have already sunk one of the enemy's warships."

"Talk seriously," said the brave and daring Maki, blushing.

"What kind of torpedo men have we?"

"We haven't got any at present, primarily because the ship was just launched at the Ishikawajima dockyards at Yokohama. Actually, I have only one torpedo man—a warrant officer with a first-class rating."

Ishikawajima Shipyard, October 1926 launch of Destroyer No. 30. *Library of Congress* (LC-B2-5259-15a)

Japanese War Fantasy

Ishikawajima Shipyard
The Ishikawajima Shipyard was a keystone in the foundation of modern Japan's industrial capability, having been founded in 1853 under the Tokugawa Shogunate to build warships that could stand up against those of Western navies.

"The warrant officer will have charge of the forward torpedo tubes, but what about those in the rear?" asked Lieutenant Maki.

"The aft tubes will be controlled by a petty officer, perhaps some former serviceman trained in torpedo work."

"What a pity! They say that when, in the Sino-Japanese War, these brave former servicemen went to fire the latest-model 25-inch torpedoes, the torpedoes actually wept with shame," said Maki.

"However, it can't be helped if we can't get trained men for this work. Even if we can get hold of some men, think of the amount of training that will be necessary," the supply officer said harshly. Then, abruptly changing his tone, he continued, "Well, anyway, I do have a torpedo-control man, first class, available, but he has only a Seaman First Class rating."

"That's all right. What kind of a man is he? And when is he available? Where is he?" asked Lieutenant Maki.

"Why, he's at a villa in Otsu where you yourself once stopped. His name is Tsuyoshi Kawano. He is a deserter."

"What, did you say Kawano?" exclaimed Lieutenant Maki, springing to his feet. "You have captured Kawano?"

"No. He gave himself up. When he heard about the war starting, he felt compelled to surrender himself. And he voluntarily surrendered to me while I was on duty mustering in the first reservists," reported the chief of the supply section, who continued, "He said he had deserted from your ship. You know him?"

"Yes, but in regard to his desertion, I am also responsible for that," admitted the former commander of the *Nara*. "Good, I'll accept Kawano."

"Wait a minute," pointed out the supply officer. "Kawano is now a prisoner serving a sentence, and he is not supposed to be released immediately for duty on a ship."

"What you say is reasonable," replied Maki, "but I believe that if the commander in chief were pressed on this matter, he would accord as considerate a treatment to a seaman first class as he did to an errant lieutenant when he restored my rank and my command."

CHAPTER 3
The Hidden Emotion of a Lion

SECTION 1: USS *OKLAHOMA*

At a time when popular clamor in the United States was shrieking for action against the Japanese, one circumstance favorable to Japan was to be noted. Part of the US fleet that was ordinarily assigned to the Pacific was at that moment lazily passing through the Panama Canal en route to the Atlantic.

Americans thought that the Japanese naval officer Maki had taken that into consideration when he sank USS *Houston*. But, according to the testimony of Lieutenant Maki at his court martial, that officer had not thought that far ahead when he made his attack. Furthermore, as rioting in Cuba had again broken out four or five days before the occurrence of the Woosung Affair, the United States could not avoid ordering naval vessels from the Pacific to Cuba to observe the trend of conditions there.

However, the revolution in Cuba failed to follow precedent and burn itself out in ten days, two weeks, or even after a month. It continued to grow in violence, further endangering American lives and property. Therefore, not only were the United States ships that had been sent to observe the situation there not withdrawn, but, on the contrary, it was necessary to increase the strength of the landing parties to protect the rights and interests of American nationals in Cuba. The real reason for the American government's irresolute attitude toward Japan during the Woosung Affair was that its entire attention was consumed by this troublesome affair in Cuba.

However, Congress finally declared war on Japan, and it became urgent for the fleet detachment in Cuba to join the main fleet for action against Japan as soon as possible. This movement would be imperative in the event that some accident might befall the Panama Canal connecting the Atlantic and Pacific Oceans, in which case the fleet detachment in Cuban waters would have to make a long detour of 13,000 sea miles to join the main fleet in San Francisco harbor. Also, even though it was unlikely that Japanese

US base at Guantanamo Bay, Cuba, 1936. *Naval Historical Center (UA 571.15)*

ATLANTIC FLEET
Guantanamo Bay

military forces would attack the Panama Canal, the Panamanian coasts being well guarded by forts with huge 14- and 16-inch guns, mine fields, and submarines, while squadrons of aircraft and strong army forces guarded the zone itself, the danger existed that some unexpected damage might be done by Japanese spies or other nationals. In any event, it was decided to get the fleet through the canal as quickly as possible.

"The army arrives tomorrow at 1 p.m. to relieve us, and we'll pull out of here at once," stated the senior naval officer, Captain Wood of USS *Oklahoma*, to the assembled commanders of the other naval ships riding at anchor off Havana.

"Allowing three hours to be consumed in making the transfer to the army, the fleet will sail at 4 p.m. We should reach Colon the day after to-morrow, at 8 a.m., if we proceed at the high speed of 15 knots. The program for the passage of the canal is set forth here," continued the captain, passing to each of the ship commanders a slip with instructions typed in purple ink. "While the responsibility for security during the fleet's passage of the canal rests with the army, I want antiaircraft batteries on all ships manned at that

USS *Oklahoma* transiting the Panama Canal, October 1936. *Naval Historical Center (NH UA 54.02.01)*

 Japanese War Fantasy

time for protection against air attack, since enemy aircraft could appear and attack the locks or the ships en route through the canal. I wish that every measure be taken for protection against such a contingency."

It was not believed that the clever Japanese had yet dispatched an aircraft carrier to the vicinity of the canal since hostilities commenced. However, Japanese aircraft could be concealed in nearby Costa Rica, Colombia, or the Republic of Panama. It was not improbable that such aircraft might make a bombing attack on the canal. The reconnaissance and attack planes of the army forces guarding the canal would be, of course, the logical means of meeting the attacks of such Japanese aircraft, but it was incumbent upon the naval vessels to protect themselves from air attacks, too.

As planned, the battleships *Oklahoma* and *Nevada*, the cruisers *Pensacola* and *Salt Lake City*, and eight destroyers departed from Havana harbor the following day at 4 p.m. These twelve men-of-war, which had been following the situation in Havana for more than forty days, then proceeded through the Gulf of Mexico and the Caribbean Sea. The commander's pennant, flown by Captain Wood of the leading ship, *Oklahoma*, fluttered in the breeze.

"Captain, we have one deserter," reported the ship's adjutant to *Oklahoma*'s captain as he stood on the bridge after the ship had cleared Havana harbor. "He is the captain's striker—that Negro."

"He is an irresponsible fellow," the old captain barked.

"I suppose that he is with that girl Shiko again."

The captain was accustomed to a desertion rate varying between 700 in the best years and 2,000 in the worst and was wont to pay little heed to only one or two desertions. On the contrary, he considered such a negligible number as grounds for congratulations.

"The poor morals existing in places such as Havana cause us lots of trouble," he exclaimed, his face assuming an expression indicating that he was at peace with the world.

The Negro boy in question, whose black face presented the same expression in moments of anger, grief, or shame, yesterday, after the departure of the ships' captains from the meeting on *Oklahoma*, had found a piece of paper with purple typewriting on the captain's desk, where it had been forgotten. He had eagerly read it, repeating over and over to himself, "*Oklahoma* . . . passage through the Gatun Locks at 10:30 a.m." Sighing with relief, he beamed at the knowledge that no one had observed him.

SECTION 2: PANAMA CANAL

The sun beat down pitilessly upon the little fleet bound from Havana when it entered Limon Bay, having emerged from the Caribbean Sea and passed the lighthouse at the entrance to the Panama Canal. White-clad sailors, scattered about the decks, were busy throwing out tow lines, using fenders, and preparing the antiaircraft guns for action. A message had previously been received by radio to the effect that the canal was prepared to handle the fleet upon arrival. Furthermore, all passage of other ships through the canal had been halted since morning. In order to facilitate the passage of the fleet as quickly as possible to the Pacific, everyone along the entire channel of 80 kilometers was on the alert.

USS *Oklahoma* transiting the Panama Canal, 1936. *Naval Historical Center (NH UA 54.02.01)*

Japanese War Fantasy

Shortly before 9 a.m., the leading vessel, *Oklahoma*, began passage of the canal. Captain Wood, standing under a tent on the bridge of the ship, wiping his red face with a handkerchief in the hot winds, said as he took on the pilot, "This is the thirteenth time I have passed through this canal. Until this time, however, I didn't properly appreciate the value of the canal."

"Thirteen times, you say? That's an unlucky omen!" The pilot, who, like all sailors, hated the number 13, swallowed hard as he said this, then continued, "However, since, as you say, the canal has been specially prepared for this passage, it may be all right, at that."

"Yes, I think so," said the captain, briefly, and then continued, "I remember, when I was a child, at the time of the Spanish-American War, the 13,000-ton battleship *Oregon* was in San Francisco harbor. That occasion was the exact opposite of this affair. The battleground was in the Atlantic then, and the ship had to make the long trip of 15,000 sea miles around the southern tip of South America. A trip like that consumed, in truth, some sixty days."

"It's nice that nowadays it takes only about eight or nine days to make the run from Havana to San Francisco."

What they said was the truth. This greatly used waterway, which America had constructed at a cost of eight years' labor and the vast sum of $500,000,000, had, like the tiger's cub, developed into this important canal.

> **Panama Canal**
> Construction of the Panama Canal cost $375,000,000 when it opened in 1914 ($7,163,750,000 in 2021 dollars).

"It depends on how you look at it, as to whether this canal is a good thing or not. It's the first thing that an enemy will consider!" the captain said. "You have not had any news in regard to the movements of the enemy fleet, have you?"

"There is a rumor that enemy submarines have arrived in Balboa Sea and are awaiting an opportunity to harass the canal."

"That's not so! The 5½-inch guns of the Japanese submarines cannot reach the canal from there. Even if they succeeded in coming in closer than the range of the big guns here, they probably could not avoid the mine fields we've laid."

"No. That's not it. Everybody is afraid that airplanes from the Japanese submarines will come and bomb the canal from the air. Say, look at that!" said the pilot suddenly, pointing at a formation of three attack planes in the sky over Gatun Locks. "Those are US Army planes. For some time now, the army has been sending out aircraft for protection from the air."

"Our preparations for defense against enemy planes are complete aboard this ship," remarked the captain, referring to the battle arrangements on his ship and pointing to the ship's antiaircraft guns. "Our greatest precautions are taken against enemy bombers that may be hidden in unknown places on land, and not those that the submarines may carry. Large bombers cannot be carried on submarines."

Illustration of the explosion aboard USS *Oklahoma*. Illustration by Katsuichi Kabashima in *Nichibei-sen Miraiki. University of Maryland Prange collection*

US Army Air Corps began patrolling sea approaches to the Panama Canal during World War I. Martin NBS-1 aircraft surveil the Pacific near Fort Amador, ca. 1927. *Library of Congress (HABS CZ,1-PANCI.V,1-1)*

From the entrance of the canal to the Gatun Locks, there is a straight stretch of 8 sea miles. The ship proceeded through this without stopping and entered the Gatun Locks shortly before 10 a.m.

The Gatun Locks are the most vital part of the canal because at this point, ships that have come up the canal from the Atlantic are raised 85 feet above sea level (or, on the contrary, ships coming from the north are lowered 85 feet to the sea level of the Atlantic). In the middle of the locks, running lengthwise, is a thick concrete partition by which the lock is divided into two waterways, one on the right and one on the left. When *Oklahoma* entered the channel on the right, the water gate behind her was shut, and the large pumping station began to sing. The water level rose as you looked at it, and the ship was raised and ready to start forward. When the water in the second lock reached the same level, the next gate was opened, and the ship was towed along by electric engines running on tracks on the banks on both sides. The distance between the ship and the banks was very narrow, being only six feet on each side.

Leaving the work mainly to the pumping station and the electric engines, the pilot began to chat with the captain. "Isn't the plan for this fleet to proceed to San Francisco, then, unless circumstances change, to Pearl Harbor, and then to lead the advance against the enemy?"

"Hmmm. We are strictly forbidden to discuss the movements of the fleet," replied the captain. "Japanese spies are everywhere, and it would be extremely serious if they got information about our movements."

"Don't toy with me," growled the pilot angrily. "I'm a real American, a descendant of ancestors who came over on the *Mayflower*. You positively need have no fear that I may be a Japanese spy."

"I was only joking. However, because the United States is a 'melting pot' in which all nationalities are mingled together, it is very risky to talk about secret matters. At the time of the recent world war, for instance, United States citizens of German extraction were very active on behalf of their mother country."

The clock under the ship's bridge clanged five times.

"Half past ten?" asked the pilot, at the same time looking at his wristwatch. He continued, "There are more than 350,000 Japanese in the United States, who are certainly not going to remain inactive. Probably they will try to do something terrible. For this reason, the authorities are keeping a sharp watch throughout America. However, just at the moment, the Negroes in the United States are running riot much more than the Japanese."

Gatun Locks of the Panama Canal, 1936. *Library of Congress (LC 6a23906r)*

"Negroes?" the captain suddenly recalled his colored boy who had deserted at Havana. He said, "Is that so? Why, we have Negroes on this ship. I wonder . . . ?"

Becoming silent, the captain strained his ears to listen. From the interior of the ship, a dull explosion sounded.

"That seemed to come from the stern," said the chief gunnery officer, who was standing at the side of the captain. "Just a moment. I'll go and see what it was," he said as he descended the aft iron ladder.

The explosion, with a noise like some prehistoric monster, was roaring under decks in the stern of the ship.

"It's the powder magazine," yelled the chief gunnery officer as he ran, accompanied by Captain Wood.

"Quick, gunnery officer, flood the magazine!"

Clouds of dark brown smoke poured from the aft hatches, skylights, and port holes. White-clad sailors, yelling excitedly, dashed madly for the fore part of the ship. Almost instantaneously, the stern half of the ship was completely hidden by smoke.

It seemed as if the flames had now crawled throughout the ship below the decks. If they should reach the magazines of the 36-centimeter gun turrets in the aft part of the vessel, the fate of the ship would be sealed. Could the chief gunnery officer open the flooding valves in time to stop the spread of the fire?

African American sailors, ca. 1920s. *Naval Historical Center (NH 56659)*

The captain, the navigator, the pilot, and all the personnel who had been on the bridge stood stiffly erect awaiting the report of the chief gunnery officer. A white-clad figure, who seemed to be the chief gunnery officer, could be seen in the smoke in the vicinity of the boat deck. He called out in a loud voice, "The flooding valves are open!"

It was not only the captain who was greatly relieved to hear this news. Several hundred of the crew also heard the words of the chief gunnery officer. Nine men had died. However, either by fate or fortune, at this moment an explosion roared from the forward turrets with a force that seemed to split the heavens: "BOOM!"

Debris flew everywhere. The captain only had time to yell, "OH!" when the bridge, stacks, boats, masts, and hundreds of white-uniformed crewmen were blown high into the air.

The havoc wrought by the explosion! Not only was the ship entirely blown to pieces, but both banks of the canal were obliterated. The electric engines and pumping machinery had disappeared completely without a trace, and even the steel dams of the water gates were blown skyward by the blast's insatiable force.

"Terrible! Terrible!" screamed the canal personnel, driven almost insane by the disaster. "The water of Gatun Lake is flowing out!"

The dam had been cut, and the water of Gatun Lake was pouring down 85 feet, like a waterfall, roaring through the waterways of the canal to Limon Bay. "Oh! Oh! The people!"

Some ten survivors of *Oklahoma* came floating along on a piece of wreckage. But the water churned so violently that there was no man ashore who could enter the stream at that time, no matter how brave he might be.

USS *Oklahoma*
In real life, USS *Oklahoma* was torpedoed and sunk at Pearl Harbor on December 7, 1941, with the loss of 429 lives.

A company of engineers from the canal garrison was hastily dispatched to the scene in response to urgent calls for help. However, they could do nothing. The water continued to flow out of the lake, day and night, all this day, and the next, and the day following that. In the end, Gatun Lake ran dry, with its bottom completely exposed to view.

As the water level of the canal was higher than sea level, it was no longer possible to raise and lower ships by means of the dangerously weakened locks. The destruction of one lock of the great Panama Canal had destroyed its marvelous power, like robbing a fairy of its magic feather robe.

After the water had gushed out of the Gatun Locks, the pitiful hulk of *Oklahoma* was exposed to view. It was difficult to realize that this wreck, with its steel decks torn off like paper and its ribs exposed like a skeleton, only three days previously had been the mighty battleship *Oklahoma*, bravely projecting American strength to all the world. Of the 1,000 men who had composed her crew, it was impossible to tell exactly how many had escaped alive. Although, happily, there were some who escaped with their lives, the great number of survivors were so critically hurt that they would never again have full use of their bodies.

The news of *Oklahoma*'s sinking was immediately transmitted to *Nevada* and the other ships of the fleet waiting in readiness in Limon Bay. An intensive search was conducted of the powder magazines on the battleship *Nevada* and cruisers *Pensacola* and *Salt Lake City*, and it is rumored that efficient time bombs, which had been concealed by parties unknown, were found in all the magazines.

"It's a conspiracy of the Japs!"

"It's the work of spies!"

Thus said the officers after exhaustively examining every member of the crews individually. Although it was claimed that it was a Japanese plot, nothing to substantiate this allegation was discovered. The only thing that was learned was that Negro sailors had deserted from every one of the ships of the fleet upon its departure from Havana.

One week after this occurrence, the president of the United States, exercising his absolute powers, issued an order to the effect that "No Negroes can serve in either the army or navy of the United States." The result of this was that the already existing shortage of personnel in the navy was aggravated, and the number of sailors was greatly decreased.

SECTION 3: USS *PATOKA*

Mare Island Navy Yard, California, 1936. Aircraft carrier USS *Langley* (CV-1) is docked at bottom center. *Naval Historical Center (NH 69002)*

The greatest base of operations of the United States fleet for action against Japan was located 3,300 sea miles north of Panama at Mare Island Naval Shipyard in San Francisco Bay. The battle fleet, comprising about half of the United States naval vessels and composed of the 16-inch (40-centimeter) gunships *Maryland, Colorado,* and *West Virginia* and the 14-inch (36-centimeter) gunships *California, Tennessee,* and *Idaho,* etc., were alternately lying alongside the docks

USS *Macon* conducting operations with two Curtiss F9C-2 Sparrowhawks over New Jersey, 1933. *Naval Historical Center (80-G-441983)*

and taking on quantities of black oil. In the offing, slightly separated from the battle fleet, the great hulks of aircraft carriers *Lexington* and *Saratoga* floated like ghosts. Close at hand, the giant dirigible *Macon* floated, moored to a mast on her mother ship, *Patoka,* and could be seen from Golden Gate Park.

USS *Patoka* near Pensacola, 1927. *Naval Historical Center (NH 60284)*

 Japanese War Fantasy

USS *Patoka* and USS *Macon*
USS *Patoka* (AO-9) was a fleet oiler that was modified to serve as a tender for US Navy airships, mounting a distinctive 100-foot-tall mooring mast. USS *Macon* (ZRS-5) was a rigid, helium-filled airship launched in March 1933. *Macon* carried a handful of parasite scout planes and a crew of sixty sailors and served as an airborne aircraft carrier.

"They are preparing to attack the land of Mount Fuji."

"Isn't it thought-provoking, fellows, that there is no way in which we can make an end of those ships right now?"

The speakers conversed in English, but, judging from their faces, there was no doubt that they were Japanese. They were, in fact, the American Japanese Frank Kodama, George Takahashi, and Henry Baba.

"You must not say things like that, even in front of American Japanese," said Frank Kodama, the oldest of the group. "Say, Jimmy Takada told me this today . . . He said, 'We second-generation fellows are real American citizens, and we must be loyal to America. If we discover any of our associates plotting harm against the United States, we should unhesitatingly notify the police at once.'"

"Let the fellows do that who want to," said Henry Baba.

"Anyway, as far as I am concerned, I don't intend to stand twiddling my thumbs when my native mother country faces defeat!"

"Look what wonderful work the Negroes did in Panama. Then look at what we, true Japanese with pure Japanese blood in our veins, have done—nothing!"

Hearing the approaching footsteps of a policeman, Frank Kodama drew in his breath sharply. When the policeman saw the three men, he gave them a side glance, then walked on.

"Say, I . . ." said George Takahashi, the youngest of the group, pointing to the aircraft carriers, "I wish I could do away with that damned *Macon*."

Kodama nudged him with his elbow and said, "That is the only one they have, and you could not get near her. However, Japan has no ship like her."

"I can't help it. I would like to set her on fire or blow her up."

"You are a fool, Henry." The young man laughed, and continued, "Why, they don't use a gallon of hydrogen gas in American airships."

"Is that so? They use helium, don't they?"

"It therefore seems to me that the only way would be to drop a bomb on her from above and then she would crash. But we are not able to do that!"

With vexed faces, the three stared at the airship, floating only a hundred feet above the water in the distance. For the second time, the policeman, emerging from the shade of eucalyptus trees, passed by the three young men. Looking at the retreating form of the policeman, Frank Kodama remarked in a serious tone, "Let's do what George suggested just now, by all means. Charlie Azuma has a plane. As for a bomb, if we go to see Mister Cho, the Chinese gambler, he'll get us one for cheap!"

"Who'll operate the plane?" Baba asked.

"We will make Charlie fly it."

"Do you think he will let us use it?"

"The important thing is money," said Kodama. He went on, "As I have a scheme for raising the money, Henry, you go to see Charlie. And you, George, come along with me to Boss Cho's place."

After Henry had gotten out of sight, Frank whispered something in George's ear. Frank jumped to his feet.

"Do you think you can really do that? Even if you exercise the greatest caution, it looks really difficult."

"Did I not read of such a thing in a book? George, in the world war there was a tale told about an Italian officer who stealthily entered an enemy navy yard and sank a battleship."

Battleship Sabotage

The speaker is probably referring—mistakenly—to two suspected incidents of Austro-Hungarian sabotage against Italian battleships: the August 2, 1916 sinking of *Leonardo da Vinci* in Taranto harbor and the September 27, 1916 sinking of *Benedetto Brin* in Brindisi harbor. At the time, a very effective, easily concealed, binary incendiary device was in wide use by Austro-Hungarian and German saboteurs.

"Is that so?" remarked George with wonderment. "But what you just said—what you intend to do—was not true, was it, Frank?"

"It's nothing out of the ordinary," answered the older man. "Suppose that we can't get Azuma's plane, we still have to do something, don't we? We might as well try my plan first without first waiting to find out what Azuma will say."

"Suppose we do follow Henry's plan. Who will you get to help you?"

"I think that we had better do it ourselves. You can't trust anybody else in a thing like this. As for those other fellows, I think they are no better than dogs!"

SECTION 4: SABOTAGE

Frank and George gave a sigh of relief after they had shoved the boat away from the bank without being observed by anyone. In the sky, neither stars nor moon could be seen. The black clouds, piled up deeply in the sky, seemed about to begin to rain at any moment.

"The weather seems made-to-order for our purposes."

"See how the engine sounds. It's more important than anything else that it not make too much noise." The two men thus chatted happily at the lucky way things had turned out.

Nevertheless, their circumstances were not perfect. Pitch darkness shrouded the sea and would probably prevent detection of their little boat, but, at the same time, the gloom hid their objective, the mother ship *Patoka* to which the dirigible was moored.

"I thought positively that this was the right direction, but . . ." remarked Frank in an uncertain voice a few moments after shoving off from the shore.

Looking backward, George remarked, "Say, Frank, guide by the lights on shore. Don't you think you should go a little more to the right?"

While saying this, George looked around to locate the Fairmont Hotel on a hill in the city, the ferry building overlooking the water, and the lights of Oakland across the bay. However, he was not absolutely sure that he could positively identity these landmarks. The amateur boatmen passed a number of yachts and motorboats floating lazily in the Sunday stillness. They figured that if they could cross San Francisco Bay, which did not extend 6 or 7 miles in an east and west direction, that they could reach the broad Pacific, where they would be safe from capture or arrest.

"Ah! It's beginning to rain," snorted George, crouching in the bow and staring intently ahead. As he announced the rain, he looked back and noted that the lights of San Francisco Bay had become completely enveloped in the mist.

"Say, isn't it cold!" hissed Frank Kodama, gnashing his teeth as the large rain drops, blown in all directions, struck the boat.

As the rain settled down to a steady downpour, their fields of vision were again restricted, and they could see nothing except the two strong beams of light on their left concentrated outside Golden Gate Bay by the ghostly searchlights of the Presidio.

The Presidio

The Presidio had been the nerve center of defense for the western United States for nearly half a century. In March 1942, from his headquarters in the Presidio, Lt. Gen. John L. DeWitt would order the internment of more than 110,000 people of Japanese ancestry because of fear of sabotage and espionage.

"Why, it is half-past three already," said Kodama, the steersman, as he glanced at the luminous dial of his wristwatch. Another hour passed as they cruised blindly around at slow speed.

"We were fools not to bring a compass or a night glass with us," grumbled Kodama finally, wearied from the long searching about.

"The next time, we will make better preparations," said George despondently. "How about giving up and going home now?"

"It's too bad, but I guess we'll have to. If day breaks while we are fooling around like this, it will be dangerous."

Kodama pulled the rudder sharply and steered on the searchlights at the Presidio. As they approached what they took to be the wharf in San Francisco, George, who was crouched in the bow of the boat, whispered in a low but sharp voice, "Frank! The Harbor Police!"

Without hesitation, Kodama pulled the steering wheel completely around to the left, at the same time straining his eyes to see through the darkness. What was this! A large black shape like a fortress wall loomed up in front of his black eyes.

"It's the aircraft carrier!" George shouted, as the towering black shape disappeared behind them. He continued, "The *Patoka* we've been looking for should be somewhere around here."

Kodama recalled instantly that *Patoka* was moored near their target, the *Macon*, and instinctively began to gesture. He gnashed his teeth in uncontrollable rage.

Ten minutes later, when the black shape of the dirigible appeared in sight overhead, they became completely calm. After putting a hammer, a short-handled marlin spike, and a pair of pliers in the pockets of their rain-coats, they removed their shoes. They clenched their right fists and struck themselves on the chest two or three times. Then, completely regaining their composure, they felt keyed up to face any danger.

USS *Patoka* with a moored airship (USS *Los Angeles*, ZR-3), off the coast of Panama, ca. February 1931. *Naval Historical Center (NH 73285)*

After that, the two could not talk any more. In silence, they manipulated the steering apparatus, stopped the engine, and took out the mooring rope. As they were attempting to make the mooring rope fast to the stern of the aircraft carrier, they were surprised to see a motor launch, which apparently belonged to the ship, tied to the Jacob's ladder hanging from the stern of the ship. Peeping through a hole in the canvas cover, they spied two mem-bers of the crew, wrapped in blankets, sleeping soundly in the dim glimmering light of the night.

"Take care not to wake them," whispered Frank in George's ear. "They'll come after us if we do!"

USS *Macon*, ca. 1933. Illustration by Katsuichi Kabashima in *Nichibei-sen Miraiki*. University of Maryland Prange collection

George Kodama stealthily climbed up the Jacob's ladder to the poop deck. The watch was probably guarding the gangways, while the signal man was undoubtedly on duty on the bridge. In addition to the good luck of not having any of the watch on the stern, still another stroke of good fortune favored these Japanese. Due to the rainstorm, everybody from the watch to the signal man had taken refuge under cover, thus leaving the decks deserted.

"This rain is a real blessing," said Frank, thanking heaven for their good luck. With more vigilance than ever, and paying the closest attention in every direction, he started to climb the steps of the mooring mast to which the huge airship was attached.

When he started to climb the mooring mast, he found that it was much higher than he had thought and was forced to stop and rest twice on the way up. Each time he paused to rest, he carefully observed the forward bridge and aft deck, but, except for the noise of the wind and rain, the ship was completely silent.

As he climbed the mooring mast, the great shape of the dirigible swayed like a ghost in the wind. Before setting out on this expedition, Frank and George had studied various technical books to ascertain exactly how the sharp nose of a dirigible was attached to a mooring mast. This research now stood Frank in good stead, for when his hand, groping around in the darkness, touched the metal fitting of the mooring mast, he knew at once what it was.

"Yes, this is it, all right," he grumbled as his hand felt around on the metal fitting of the mast in the cold rain. "It is constructed like a railway train coupling."

Japanese War Fantasy

If the pin is withdrawn and the coupling struck once lightly with a hammer, the mooring apparatus should be released, he thought. However, on investigation, Frank found that, in this case, within the big pin there was another smaller pin that was firmly soldered to the larger one. As a result of this, his work consumed an unexpectedly long time. However, after he had removed the lead and solder form the smaller pin, everything worked fine.

When only one connection remained, Frank noticed that his right hand, in which he held the hammer and which he had raised to sever this last link, was trembling uncontrollably. He became frightened when he realized that, if he struck this blow with his hammer, he would send this great dirigible in front of him sailing off over the distant sea to an unknown destination.

Glancing down to the stern of the ship, he could see a black shape that he knew to be George, who seemed to be calling out something such as, "What are you waiting for?"

Closing his eyes, he gathered the strength in his right arm. He thought that he heard two or three shots fired one after the other in the neighborhood of the carrier and realized that he did not have a second to waste. He swung his right arm down smartly and struck the coupling, severing it with one blow, whereupon the huge *Macon* immediately drifted away.

"Well! I have finished her!" declared Frank in a voice that evoked à great stress lifted from his mind, as the great oblong shape of the dirigible disappeared into the darkness of the southwest.

This exuberance at the complete success of the venture was slightly premature. Frank idled a considerable time after cutting the *Macon* loose and had just descended three or four steps of the mooring mast when he again heard what he thought to be a rifle shot from the direction of the ship's stern. Suddenly, a piercing bugle call rang out from the ship's bridge.

"I can't reach the boat now," said Frank to himself as he looked down on the deck and saw human forms running around everywhere. "There is no way around it. I must act like a man, or perhaps like an 'American Japanese,'" he thought.

Ni'ihau Incident

Fukunaga's tale of Frank Kodama, George Takahashi, and Henry Baba reveals an expectation by Japanese nationalists that "American Japanese" might feel compelled to commit subversion in case of war with the US. The Ni'ihau incident in December 1941 may be the only example of such sedition. A Zero damaged in the Pearl Harbor attack crashed onto the isolated Ni'ihau Island, where the pilot, Shigenori Nishikaichi, assisted by three Hawaiians of Japanese descent, terrorized the Ni'ihauans for six days.

Five minutes later, a brilliant beam from a searchlight revealed Frank Kodama halfway down the mooring mast. Ten minutes after this, Frank and the wounded George Takahashi lay together upon the deck, securely bound.

Grumman F2F-1s of USS *Ranger* squadron VF-3 over California, ca. June 1937. *Naval Historical Center (NH 83928)*

The naval station was in a din of commotion from top to bottom. On all the ships, the cry went up, "It's an attack by Japanese submarines!" and the crews were mustered to their battle stations, where they prepared the big guns for action. Later, when the real facts became clear, ten powerful searchlights were brought into action to pierce the darkness and search the skies. Notwithstanding these measures, and the fact that reconnaissance planes from the neighboring carriers and destroyers with searchlights were dispatched in the rain outside the Golden Gate, no trace of the great dirigible was ever found.

CHAPTER 4
Big Brother and Little Brother

SECTION 1: TOKAIDO EXPRESS

The Tanna Tunnel was finally opened to traffic. In all the hot-spring spas and excursion resorts along the main Tokaido Railway Line and the Atami Railway Line, houses for rent became very scarce and the price of land rose precipitously. Only one place, Manazuru, was avoided. Trains crowded with passengers passed it without stopping. The reason for this was that Manazuru did not have hot springs, and people overlooked its merits.

Tanna Tunnel
The Tanna Tunnel became a symbol of national pride when it opened in 1934. The shaft's construction was an epic engineering achievement that took seventeen years and claimed at least sixty-seven workmen's lives as crews bored nearly 5 miles through the perilous Hakone Mountains in Shinzuoka Prefecture, a region of active volcanoes and frequent earthquakes.

However, from the standpoint of picturesque beauty and grandeur, it is probably so that the neighborhood of Manazuru was the most splendid in all Japan. Since Japan is the most famous country in the world for scenic beauty, its various famous places have, since ancient times, been known to many people. In some respects, we cannot admire the fuss that these famous places make about scenery. From the point of grandeur, ever since olden times, Kantan Bay at Beppu has been long recognized as the best. While at that place there is no level and open scenery, there is the utmost variety to be observed in the shape of its mountains, the forms of its creeks, and the color of the sea surrounding it.

The artist Miyagi introduced to the world the beauties of Manazuru. This painter gave the name Japanese Riviera to the belt of country, with its scenic beauty, saying it was a carbon copy of the Riviera region of the Inland Sea.

Manazuru
Manazuru, in Kanagawa Prefecture, is an ancient town of renowned beauty thrusting into Sagami Bay on a crane-shaped peninsula.

The young, amateur wireless engineer Mr. Yaginuma was completely entranced by this region the first time he laid eyes upon it. But the real reason for his enchantment with this place was complicated. Drawn by the awe-inspiring grandeur of the Japanese Riviera, he visited the region and found on one of its mountains the Japanese navy radio communications school. He struck up acquaintance with some of the naval personnel of the school, and, through the bond of friendship thus cemented, he quickly discovered a suitable place where he himself could work at radio. Eventually, he built a private radio station with the call letters JVD on a small hill in the region.

Having been left a fortune by his parents, Mr. Yaginuma could not bring himself to devote time to any kind of serious study until he discovered radio. From that time on, he became greatly enamored with radio and wireless machines. Mr. Yaginuma had no time for anything else and was so enthusiastic about his wireless work that he would even get up in the middle of the night to listen to messages coming in over his radio set.

"Do you have to go already?" inquired the young proprietor of station JVD. "Why not stay here with me?" His sailor guest had climbed down the mountain from the naval radio school to pay him a visit and had risen to go when the clock struck eleven. "You should stay a while. I still have something to tell you," he continued.

"Well, to tell the truth, I am off duty tonight," said the sailor, sitting down again. "What is it that you want to tell me?"

"It's about the war," said Yaginuma. "I have not heard any news of the war since a month after it started. Where is the American fleet now? What is the Japanese fleet going to try to do to oppose the American fleet?"

"Didn't you see in the newspapers four or five days ago that the American expeditionary fleet, which was being assembled at San Francisco and San Pedro, had sailed for Hawaii? As to Japan's actions, we have seized Guam, and, as you undoubtedly know, our army is now cooperating with the navy in an attack on the Philippines."

"I know that much already! There was not the least chance of the Philippines not falling, of course. So, what is our fleet doing now?"

"Why, we do not know anything about what they are doing!" said the naval radio man. "They are afraid of spies and keep things such as that secret. I wonder where they will strike next."

True to his reputation as an amateur, the faint buzzing sound of the microphone on the desk did not escape his ears.

"That's a signal, isn't it?" Then, returning to the original subject, the sailor asked, "Where do you think the navy will strike next?"

Mr. Yaginuma, noting the signal, manipulated the radio set's direction indicator and found that the signal was coming from the southeast.

"To the southeast from here, there are only land-sending radio stations, but it is possible that this signal may be coming from some special station at sea," he muttered. Just then, another signal, now dim, now loud, could be heard.

"This signal is being sent by the same code as the other one we just heard," said the sailor. "What direction is it coming from?"

"Direction?" asked Yaginuma, as he again manipulated the direction-detecting apparatus. "South, the extreme south. Isn't it some sort of a signal from a navy guard ship?"

"No, you are mistaken," said the navy radio man, leaning his head toward the set. "This is rather queer."

The sailor opened the glass doors that faced south and with Yaginuma went out on the balcony, where they both stared intently in the direction of the black sea. They noted two or three lights on the sea, which they took to be fishing boats. An orange-colored flash in the offing to the left of the fishing-boat lights attracted their attention. At first, they thought that this light was a pine torch lit by some fishermen. Just then, a long, drawn-out, weird, and uncanny wail shattered the quiet of the night. Before they had the time to think, a terrific explosion, which sent up a large flame, occurred right under their eyes on the beach near Nebu River.

"That's an enemy ship!" yelled the sailor. "It's an attack by an enemy submarine!"

Yaginuma excitedly ran for his telescope. Just as he returned to the balcony, the second shell was fired, uncanny sounding, from the offing.

The second shot, which fell in about the same place as the first, appeared to strike a hut-like structure on the beach, and the building burst into flames. In the light of the flames, Yaginuma watched through his telescope as fishermen, women, and children fled wildly from the burning building. Although it was night, owing to the great distance from his house he could not hear the voices of the people on the beach. However, the figures appeared so large through the telescope that he could almost imagine that he could hear their agonized cries.

At this moment, the two men again became cognizant that the transmitter of the radio was broadcasting. Although, as before, the signals were still faint, they could clearly make them out this time.

"Dot dash dash dot dot dot," went the instrument.

"S-400?" asked Yaginuma, inclining his head. "I wonder what the meaning of that is . . . ?"

"'Short 400' means 400 yards under. It is a ranging signal," answered the navy man. "There is some fellow in communication with the enemy who is spotting shots for him."

Just then, two flashes flared up at sea in the offing. Taking the interval from the watch, they noticed that there were about five seconds between flashes and that, less than thirty seconds after the last flash, two explosions occurred on the upper part of the cliff. Then the transmitter again sounded out a series of dots and dashes.

"'Over 100,' 100 yards over. That's what that reads. It is disgraceful!"

For the third time, the atmosphere of the Japanese Riviera was split by a terrific concussion while the orange-colored light flooded the offing. Then, immediately after the wireless transmitter had sounded "OK, OK, OK," the wild firing began again. In describing the affair the next day, the morning newspapers in Tokyo stated: "Special dispatch from Odawara. An amateur radio engineer, Mr. Yaginuma, declared the following in an interview: 'The bombardment lasted more than ten minutes, and all the shots struck in one place. At first, I wondered what they were aiming at, and couldn't figure it out. So, I got my telescope and exerted all efforts to locate where the shots were falling. Then, an express train emerged from the tunnel, and the beam of its headlight cut straight toward the target area. The train kept rushing forward and disappeared from sight. I thought that this was extremely strange.'

"The sailor with me was constantly inquiring, 'How is it that the direction indicator of the radio points to a place in the southeast where there is no station equipped with a transmitter?' His words made me recall that, about five days previously, I had gone on a sketching trip with Professor Miyagi. With our kits slung on our backs, we had wandered over hill and dale searching for a suitable place to sketch. Halfway up a mountain on the coast, exactly half a kilometer southeast of my house, and hidden in a pine forest, there is a foreign-style house with a red tile roof. We had gone that day on a sketching trip, but when I noticed that a small antenna was affixed to the roof of that house, I said to myself, 'Ha! Here is another of my fraternity who seems to have a beam antenna capable of receiving messages even from far-away Australia.' The house looked suspicious to me. So, Miyagi and I, together with two sailors with drawn swords, who had come up just then through the dark mountain road, entered the house to investigate. We found a fine radio set, even better than mine, that had been kicked and battered, but there was no sign of the tenant. The only thing that was clear was that the tenant was a foreigner. This could be gathered from the chairs, tables, and bed—foreign furniture. However, when I inquired about the occupant later, at the police station, I received the answer that the house is the villa of an official of the Yokohama Phonograph Company and that they were unaware that a foreigner was living there."

Yokohama Phonograph Company
The Yokohama Phonograph Company was established in 1930 by JVC (formerly Victor Company of Japan). Foreign industrial facilities in Japan fell under suspicion as militarists expanded their political power, compelling parent company RCA Victor to sell JVC to Japanese owners in 1938. In 1945, the Yokohama plant was destroyed by US bombers.

In addition to the above interview, the newspapers commented on the rumors that an enemy submarine had escaped from Manila and that Mr. Yaginuma had seen an express train plunge from a steep precipice directly into the sea:

"Protests are being voiced everywhere at the aimless policy of the authorities, who are compelled to realize the great importance of the Tokaido Railway main line by occurrences such as this bombing and shelling of our coast by enemies from beyond the sea."

US submarines, ca. 1936, *left to right:* USS *Nautilus* (SS-168); USS *Narwhal* (SS-167); USS *Shark* (SS-174), marked P3; USS *Dolphin* (SS-169), marked D1; USS *Porpoise* (SS-172), marked P1; USS *Pike* (SS-173), marked P2; and USS *Tarpon* (SS-175), marked P4. *Naval Historical Center (NH 3036)*

However, the newspapers did not mention the fact that General Maki, commander of the newly organized Manila Expeditionary Force Headquarters, and more than seven hundred officers and men bound for the Philippines perished at the bottom of Sagami Bay when their express train was lost.

SECTION 2: ENEMY SUBMARINE

"Say, what is that cloth wrapped around the left sleeve of the captain?" asked a sailor, puffing a cigarette under the bridge of the destroyer *Kurumi.* He looked up at the form of the captain as the latter climbed up to the bridge.

"That? Why that's a mourning badge," replied a companion.

"Fool!" exclaimed the first sailor, nudging his companion with an elbow. "I know it's a mourning badge. What I wanted to know is, who is it he's mourning?"

"Why, you don't know anything, do you?" snapped the sailor who had just taken the elbow in the stomach. "The captain is in mourning for his father, of course."

"His father, the army general?"

"Yes, the one who was just appointed commanding general of the Manila Expeditionary Force. He was killed the other day in that attack by the American submarine."

"Those fellows! They certainly know whom to pick!" said the first sailor, drawing close to his companion to jab him with his elbow again. "Whereabouts was the general's transport sunk?"

"It was not at sea, fellow. It happened when the general was aboard a train."

"You're a fool, man! There isn't a navy in the world that has submarines that can launch torpedoes at railway trains!"

"That's all you know. I'll tell you how it was done. Submarines carry large guns, don't they? If a submarine with large guns were to appear in Sagami Bay, it could reach a railroad train on the Tokaido line with its guns, couldn't it? Rub your stomach well and think that over, and maybe you'll understand."

"What? Do you mean to say that the shelling incident of the other night had some connection with the general's train?" asked the elbow-jabbing sailor with round eyes.

"Certainly, there was a connection between the two things. In the first place, the general was their objective. They put spies to work in Japan who kept them informed about all his movements every minute and second of the time. They particularly wanted to get the general because he was the father of Lieutenant Maki, who started the Woosung Affair, so by killing the general they could cleverly avenge that affair!"

"Is that the truth?" replied the other, only half believing what he had heard. "There was nothing in the newspapers . . ."

"It was not put in the newspapers for fear of hurting the morale of people like you," explained the sailor. "But you ask the section chief, if you don't believe what I say. What do you say, Kawano?"

Seaman Kawano, who had been silently listening to the conversation, nodded.

They all remained silent for a short time, then the first sailor spoke again and said, "If that's so, this part of the sea is dangerous."

"How is it dangerous?"

"Because that American submarine may be hiding somewhere around here."

"Perhaps it is. Maybe that's the reason that we are convoying these transports."

Off the starboard stern, two hired army transports followed in single column at a distance of 400 meters. The convoy, with four 800-ton-class destroyers guarding it, two on the right of the transports and two on the left, was steaming southward past the eastern shore of Ojima Island in Izu Bay.

Just two steps above the chitchatting sailors, the chief surgeon paced the bridge nursing a toothpick, with which he gestured toward the transports. He inquired of the senior lieutenant, "I say, what about that baggage?"

"I have done as I was ordered," replied the lieutenant.

"That included cement, gravel, cannons, gun carriages, and materials for building fortifications, did it not?"

"With those materials, the army should be able to greatly strengthen those islands!"

"Temporarily," said the lieutenant. He explained, "If you were the American commander, the thing for which you would go first would be the Ogasawara Island Group, would it not? That group of islands is nearest to the heart of Japan and is also the most easily captured. For these reasons, those islands would make admirable places for enemy airplanes and submarines to gain a foothold."

"I don't quite understand," said the surgeon doubtfully. "If the Ogasawara Islands are so important, why have we not completely fortified them long ago? I say, it's like locking the door after the burglar has gone."

"Unfortunately, what you say is true. Under the terms of the Washington Naval Treaty relating to restrictions on fortifications, we are prohibited from adding any new fortifications to those islands until December 31 of this year."

"The army are fools, aren't they?" sneered the doctor irritably. "Imagine the Army Construction Bureau trying to start out now to build fortifications there! Why, the concrete will not have time to dry before the enemy arrives!"

"No matter what you say, the treaty prohibited it, and the situation couldn't be helped."

"Treaty or not, if it had been I, and my country's fate depended on it, I would have instantly broken the treaty!"

"Things like that do not concern you, doctor. You had better stick to

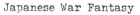

your specialty—operating on boils," quipped the senior lieutenant with a laugh. "Nevertheless, in America there are also people like you who say that if impregnable new fortifications had been built in the Philippines and Guam, Japan would be in a tight spot now."

"All right," said the doctor. Realizing that he was losing the argument, he attempted to regain lost ground by adding, "But haven't the Philippines already fallen into our hands?"

"That surprised me very much also. I thought that the Imperial Japanese Army, with its traditional bravery, should have been able to raise the Rising Sun over Manila and Corregidor within a month after the outbreak of hostilities."

Corregidor and Caballo Island in the distance, key fortified islands at the mouth of Manila Bay, ca. 1945. *Naval Historical Center (NH 12202)*

Manila and Corregidor Campaign
The actual Japanese campaign to take Manila and Corregidor lasted about five months, from December 29, 1941, until May 6, 1942.

"In my opinion, the blame rests with our navy for the loss of those army transports in attacks by enemy submarines and airplanes."

"We overtaxed ourselves, that's what we did," said the senior officer apologetically. He added, "As a matter of fact, Grand Imperial Headquarters itself exerted every effort to expedite the capture of the Philippines because they were fearful that the United States would reach Manila before we took it."

"But, Lieutenant, isn't it true that the US Atlantic Fleet could not immediately join the Pacific Fleet because the Panama Canal was blown up?"

"No matter, they could have still helped Manila . . . What I mean is that the United States has thirteen battleships in the Pacific, and those ships from the Atlantic may yet come to this part of the world," said the senior lieutenant.

At this moment, a man on the deck below yelled, "Torpedo off the port bow!"

The senior lieutenant sprang up from his folding chair and rushed to the port side to peer out, at the same time calling out, "Helm to starboard! Both engines full speed ahead! Officer on duty, sound the sirens. Signal man, stand by!"

Japanese depth charge rack and mortar, ca. 1945. *Naval Historical Center (USMC 76882)*

Japanese signalman on aircraft carrier *Junyo*, ca. 1945. Despite advances in signals technology, modern navies still needed signalmen with flags and bugles. *Naval Historical Center (NH 218541)*

The ship commander, who had been idling in the chart room below, burst onto the bridge and nodded, "Very good, lieutenant!"

In the brief span of time it took the destroyer to swing left in answer to its helm, the speeding torpedo reached a point just 20 meters from the starboard side of the ship. Just at this moment, when everyone was holding their breath in anticipation, a second report announced, "Periscope off the bow!"

The destroyer, handled by the captain, made a dash at the submarine. The periscope instantly disappeared, and the bow of the destroyer was unable to ride over the conning tower of the enemy submarine. However, the destroyer dropped four bombs from her stern into the sea.

After the bombs had sunk an undetermined depth into the sea, they exploded, causing mountains of water to be thrown above the surface. When the sea had subsided, its entire surface glistened with heavy oil. The devil of the sea had met its end.

On the bridge of the destroyer *Kurumi*, a signal man with a red-and-white flag faced the captain as he signaled to the transports that the battle was over.

"The enemy submarine has positively been sunk. The discoverer of the torpedo and the enemy periscope was Seaman First Class Tsuyoshi Kawano."

SECTION 3: LIEUTENANT MAKI

Naval lieutenant Eitaro Maki was exactly thirty-three years old when he was orphaned by the death of his father, the general, in the loss of the express train in Sagami Bay. Some people said that the death of the general failed to cast a pall of gloom over the Maki residence in Tokyo at Minamicho, Aoyama, the home of Lieutenant Maki's mother, his younger brother, who was a first lieutenant in the army, and his sister, of about his brother's age. The probable reason for this, they said, was that the other members of the family were not as affected by the death as the orphan, Eitaro. However, people who made these statements did not know the inside situation of the Maki family. According to the census register at the Ward Office in Akasaka, Fumi, the forty-seven-year-old wife of the senior Eitaro Maki was the general's second wife and was not the mother of the eldest boy, Eitaro. The younger brother and younger sister, however, were the children of the general's second wife and thus were technically Eitaro's half brother and half sister.

Since Eitaro had left his father's house with his real mother when he was very young, he had only a faint remembrance of his real mother. At that time, his father was frequently absent from home for long periods. In thinking about this fact afterward, even now, Eitaro did not clearly understand things. It seemed to him that his father and mother occupied separate houses, he and his mother in one house and his father in another. He recalled that every afternoon, his mother would put him in his carriage, which was the fashionable thing to do then, and take him to some place where there was a wide-open plain. There were many soldiers riding bareback and galloping about on horses. His young mother would take him out of his carriage and, holding him tightly in her arms, would say to him, "See your father. He is riding on that horse . . ." as she gazed intently at a figure on horseback far off in the distance. He could still remember to this day how large his mother's eyes became on such occasions and how she wept and then would shove him back into the perambulator. These visits to the parade ground were like daily lessons in school, he remembered.

Shortly after this, he was taken away from his mother and placed with an old woman to be reared. When he cried and called for his mother, his father treated him good humoredly. Finally, he was told one day, "Little boy, don't cry, for, tomorrow, you will have a new mother."

Eitaro thought that his childish-faced, new mother was very young and beautiful, and he quickly became very much attached to her. After this, he gradually came to forget his original mother.

One day his new mother said to Eitaro, "Your other mother was a bad woman. She imposed on your father and you." Eitaro thought that he had better keep away from such a bad person.

He remembered that, after his brother and sister were born, he had had the reckless desire to seize an opportunity to meet his real mother again. However, he was afraid that, if he mentioned this desire to his father, he would be scolded. Also, he didn't have the courage to face his present mother and tell her this.

After he had grown up, he inquired of the old woman who had once temporarily been entrusted with his care as to where his mother was, if she had married again, or if she was dead. However, he could learn no news of his real mother from the old woman. Furthermore, this lack of knowledge about his mother was not confined to Eitaro; his father was also ignorant of what had become of her.

Thus passed twenty years.

Now his father was dead. After the funeral, when Eitaro was straightening out his father's belongings, a faded photograph of a lady with an unfamiliar face fell out of a dresser drawer. His stepmother said, "That is a picture of your real mother." He looked at the photograph a second time, but it called up no recollections from his memory except for one thing—the extreme largeness of the eyes. The general impression he got from the picture was that the lady was exactly the opposite in disposition to his cheerful and happy stepmother. Although Eitaro knew absolutely nothing of his mother's life since the time he had been taken away from her, he had not thought that his mother was as gloomy and melancholy as she appeared in this picture. People's whole lives can be affected by a single stroke of fate, but he did not believe that one's natural disposition could really be changed by any single event.

In the end, Eitaro framed the picture in a silver frame and took it back with him to his ship. There he placed it, together with one of his father in uniform, on the desk in the captain's cabin of the destroyer *Kurumi*.

SECTION 4: THE CAPTAIN AND THE SEAMAN

Seaman First Class Tsuyoshi Kawano came as far as the door of the captain's cabin, hesitated, and then, regaining his courage, knocked on the door. From within, he heard the captain, in a natural tone of voice, inquire, "What is it?"

"Did you send for me?" respectfully asked the seaman first class.

"Yes. Although I have questioned you a little already today, I would like to talk with you further," said the officer. "I have already thanked you, as captain of this ship, for the deed you did today. It is entirely owing to you, because of the quickness with which you discovered that torpedo, that this ship was saved. Then, you are also to be congratulated on the fact that you sunk that submarine so splendidly."

"Yes, sir," answered the seaman tersely, then continued, "I want to congratulate the captain particularly for the outcome of today's event."

"As to that, you are right that I am to be congratulated on this day's work. I avenged myself on my father's enemy today," the captain said, shoving forward a chair. "Here, take a seat. I want to talk to you in a leisurely fashion."

The two men sat on opposite sides of a round table in the little captain's cabin.

"I have been busy with my new duties on the trial run of this destroyer and have not had time until now to talk with you casually," said the captain. He then broached the subject that was foremost on his mind, saying, "I want to talk to you about the time when you disappeared from the destroyer *Nara*. Specifically, I would like to know your motive for deserting."

Although Kawano had not expected to be interrogated on this subject when the captain sent for him today, he was still prepared for it. When the captain raised the issue of his desertion, he recalled all his former uneasiness and anger, and his mouth stiffened. The captain spoke, saying, "Up to the time when you disappeared from the *Nara*, I secretly had confidence in you, but, for a spell after that, I hated you because I thought that you had betrayed my confidence in you. Then, I realized that if a serious man like you would desert, there must have been some valid motive that compelled you."

Kawano spoke resentfully and said, "If that's all the captain knows . . ."

"That's what I heard from the section chief. I heard that at that time you had become acquainted with a very nice young lady."

"No. You are mistaken, Captain," interrupted the sailor, stung to the quick by the commander's words. "The truth was that I went because my mother was dying, and my blood was necessary to save her life. That is the truth, Captain, and because even for that they would not give me special permission to go ashore."

"I heard a slightly different story. I heard that you were besides yourself about a certain young woman and that you left to meet her."

"That is wrong! Wrong!" the sailor pleaded. "It is true that I was in love with Chieko, but under no circumstances would I have deserted from the navy on that account."

"How did your mother's sickness turn out?"

"The blood transfusion was unsuccessful, and my mother died. At the funeral she was all alone. I heard about it afterward in talking to the nurse, and it made me detest the navy because I had not been able to be with her at the end and at her funeral," said the sailor in a scarcely audible voice as he turned his head away. "My mother was very dear to me. I don't suppose that you can understand this feeling, but . . ."

"So that was the way it was?" sighed the captain. "Kawano, I, too, have lost my mother!"

"Why, when your father died recently, I saw a picture of him together with your mother in the newspapers."

"That was my stepmother. See, here is a picture of my real mother," said the captain, reaching behind him and taking a silver-framed picture from the desk and extending it toward the sailor. "I was only four years old when I parted from her, and I have always regretted it."

After one glance at the photograph, the sailor unconsciously exclaimed, "Oh," in a faint whisper full of surprise and reached for the picture to take it from the captain's hand. His eyes widened as he gazed intently with all his soul at the picture.

"Kawano, what is it?" shot the captain in a sharp voice. "You . . . That picture . . . !"

"Why, this is my mother," remarked the sailor without raising his eyes from the faded photograph in his trembling hand. "It's my dead-and-gone mother!"

"Your mother? Why, that is my mother! She was a lady called Chise," declared the captain, his chest heaving with excitement.

In reply, Kawano removed a small photograph from inside his coat, where it had been hidden, and showed it to the captain, saying, "Yes, that's right. Your mother was named Chise, was she . . . Well, this is a picture of my mother."

The captain turned the picture over and read the inscription on the back: "Chise Yamamura, age 42." The unfortunate sailor had kept this small photograph on his person since his mother's death. Comparing it with that of his own mother, the captain saw that, although Kawano's picture was perhaps a more inferior and older photograph than his own, there could be not the slightest doubt that the person in both photographs was one and the same. The same face, flooded with feeling. The great, round eyes.

"Is that so?" finally said Eitaro Maki, drawing a long breath. "I did not know this until this minute."

Overcome by emotions, the two men sat silent for several moments. Finally, the officer rose and said softly, "Well, then we are brothers. We must work together with all our strength and accomplish brave things!"

The sailor shook hands warmly with the captain and was about to leave the cabin when the second officer entered. He said, "Captain, this is a message from the Funabashi Station. It reads, 'The battle force of the United States Fleet, less *Nevada*, *Wyoming*, and *Butte*, arrived safely at Pearl Harbor, Hawaii, yesterday, the 25th. Signed, Imperial Grand Headquarters.'"

Funabashi Station
Funabashi was the site of a detachment of the Tokyo Naval
Communications Unit of the Imperial Japanese Navy.[1]

Japanese War Fantasy

CHAPTER 5
Quick Action, Early Decision

SECTION 1: HAWAIIAN BANANAS

"Capture that island quickly," said an officer, looking through his binoculars. Diamond Head reflected in the lenses. "I want to eat bananas from those trees there."

"I would like some pineapples," answered another officer who was studying the island through his telescope. "I have forgotten completely the taste of sweet, raw pineapple."

P2Y-1 patrol aircraft of squadron VP-10 over Diamond Head, January 1934. *Naval Historical Center (NH 81663)*

Above: Japanese officers in the auxiliary port engine room of a Type I submarine (I-14), ca. 1945. *Naval Historical Center (NH 1118799)*

Left: Japanese Kadai-class submarine *I-71*, 1939. Launched in 1934, she operated from Japan's Kwajalein base in 1941–42, supporting operations against Pearl Harbor and Midway Island, then participated in the Aleutians campaign, and was sunk by depth charges from US destroyers in the Southwest Pacific in February 1944. *Naval Historical Center (NH 73055)*

Japanese War Fantasy

Three Japanese crewmen and 21-inch torpedo tubes in submarine *I-58* forward torpedo room, Sasebo, Japan, January 1946. *I-58* sank USS *Indianapolis* five months earlier. *Naval Historical Center (NH USMC 139986)*

This conversation echoed in the command post of Type I Submarine No. 44. It was part of a Japanese submarine flotilla that surrounded the island of Oahu in the Hawaiian Island Group, which lies 2,098 sea miles from San Francisco and 3,379 miles from Yokohama. At this time, Submarine No. 44 lay off the southern coast of Oahu. It was not surprising that the ordinarily patient Japanese crews of these boats were unable to control their desire for fresh food. More than twenty days had passed since the flotilla left Yokosuka, and all fresh meat, vegetables, and fruit had been exhausted. The men had had nothing to eat for breakfast, dinner, or supper but canned food and rice. Most of the officers had visited the Hawaiian Islands as naval cadets in years gone by and had vivid recollections of eating their fill of luscious island fruit, so their repugnance to the canned-food diet became almost unbearable when their boats approached the archipelago. For this reason, when the boats approached close to shore, these hungry and ba-nana-coveting men were in a fit frame of mind to drive their submarines straight ahead, without stopping, to reach the paradise for which they longed. However, the American enemy had placed no fewer than 50,000 mechanical mines in the waters around the islands as a defensive measure to prevent Japanese submarines from drawing too close.

Waikiki Beach, Hawaiian Territory, May 1935. *Naval Historical Center (2015.18.01)*

"That place over there is Waikiki Beach," said the officer who wanted bananas.

"There is a very pretty park there too."

"Yes. There is an aquarium in the park that has colorful, poisonous tropical fish."

"When we were on our navigation cruise and visited this island, a fleet of Japanese fishing boats, flying Rising Sun flags, came out to about this point to meet us," said an officer, and, with deep emotion, continued, "I wonder what the 150,000 Japanese on these islands are doing now."

"I believe that both native-born and alien Japanese on the islands are planning to unite under the Japanese flag, but they haven't any weapons."

"Anyway, I wish that we would draw in a little nearer to the shore so that we could see what the land looks like."

"Don't joke about it, man! Don't you know that when our I-type Submarine No. 19 went to put down some mines outside of Pearl Harbor, it ran into the enemy's mine barrage and received terrible punishment, even though No. 19 made absolutely no noise to give its presence away?" said the banana-craving officer.

Japanese War Fantasy

Japanese sailors sweating in the galley of a Type I submarine, ca. 1945. *Naval Historical Center (NH 111808)*

"Oh well, what shall we do? Can you see anything?"

"I'm not certain whether I see anything or not, but it looks something like a fleet of trawlers putting out."

"Indeed," said both the pineapple and banana officers, turning their glasses to shore. "Yes! It is them, finally coming out!"

The trawlers that had started out were really minesweepers. Their purpose was to open a mine-free channel by sweeping up the barrage of mines, which it was suspected that Japanese minelaying submarines had deposited. The idea seemed to be that, when a channel had been completely swept of mines, the American fleet would put out to sea, somewhat like the procedure in a well-ordered household when the master's morning departure for the office naturally follows the maid's neat placement of the shoes in the entranceway.

Trawlers, such as this fishing boat *Leslie J. Fulton*, were acquired by the US Navy and converted to minesweepers. This vessel became USS *Waxbill* in 1940. *Naval Historical Center (NH 102017)*

Japanese Custom with Shoes
MID translator's note: This refers to the orderly arrangement of Japanese clogs and sandals in the entry of homes, after such footwear has been removed by their wearers on entering the house.

An American paravane, a towed device that sliced the mooring cables of mines, is hoisted above the deck of USS *Mercury*, ca. 1919. *Naval Historical Center (NH98583)*

Between forty and fifty trawlers and destroyers maneuvered around all day long, dragging a minesweeping apparatus called a paravane. When the paravane engaged the cables attaching the mines, it severed these hawsers easily. After the anchoring cables were cut, the mines bobbed up to the surface and floated there. Then, sailors aboard the minesweeper would shoot the mines from afar with rifles, detonating them with a loud roar. The mine-clearing work continued until sundown, and a surprisingly large expanse of sea was cleaned of mines.

Japanese submarine *I-55* was a Kaidai-type boat, built in 1925, that survived until 1945. *Naval Historical Center (NH 111797)*

When night fell, the vigilant Submarine No. 44 rose to the surface so that about half of the boat's hull was above the surface, and the refreshing breeze could play on the conning tower. Only the sub commander, two officers, and the signal man stood on top of the conning tower. These men stood there silently in the night, with binoculars in hand, and watched for the sortie of the enemy fleet, which they expected any moment.

The long-awaited enemy fleet finally appeared, coming from the direction of Pearl Harbor. It was about 1:00 in the night. Several detachments of destroyers proceeded in advance and ran here and there in the pitch-black darkness, searching around like hunting dogs with their noses to the ground. Whenever they would discover a stray mine, they would explode it.

Following the destroyers came the cruisers, apparently 10,000-ton cruisers. On account of the relentlessly searching destroyers and the mine barrage, I-type Submarine No. 44 was unable to approach very closely to the emerging fleet. But although the number of enemy ships could not be definitely determined, it was certain that the number of ships in the little squadron was not as many as five or six.

"They are certainly moving fast!" said an officer to the submarine commander. He peered through the starlight as the American cruiser squadron quickly disappeared into the darkness.

"They were moving at no less than 24 knots, I think," answered the commander.

US heavy cruisers in column formation, 1936. *Naval Historical Center (NH 109478)*

"They could not move on a zigzag course at 24 knots without having shown their fangs here."

After the cruisers had disappeared, the destroyers that had preceded them returned quickly to the harbor, and the sea again returned to its original state of loneliness.

"I guess that is all for tonight," declared the commander. "The unit that has just passed is the advance guard, which will form the first line of the 'Circle Formation.'"

"What will the battleships do?"

"They will follow the cruisers at 400 or 500 miles. It will probably be tomorrow night before they start."

"Then tomorrow night will be a happy one for us!"

"At any rate, this proves that the enemy is moving to the attack of the Western Pacific."

"But if the enemy becomes lost in the Western Pacific, they will have only *Wyoming* and *Utah* left."

Japanese submarine *I-52* (later redesignated *I-152*) was a large, Kaidai-type boat, built in 1923, based upon the design of British K-class submarines of World War I. *Naval Historical Center (NH 111798)*

"The expression 'quick action, quick decision' applied to this case explains why Japan is idling around the Philippines waiting for the enemy."

"I am concerned about the Philippines," spoke up a young officer anxiously. "If these ships can somehow or other get to the Western Pacific, we'll never be able to dispose of them."

"Don't worry about that. Rather, cheer up and think about how we are going to attack and kill off two enemy battleships armed with 16-inch guns."

The following night, at a signal of the gong, fourteen cruisers, followed by thirteen capital ships, emerged from the harbor and steamed through the channel that had been cleared of mines. How carefully planned had been the enemy's preparations! The high speed of the cruisers was 24 knots, and that of the battleships 18 knots, as they moved out from Pearl Harbor through the cleared channel. Furthermore, the exit of the channel had been profusely mined by the escorting destroyer flotilla.

Nevertheless, three or four Japanese submarines, some submerged and some afloat, lay in wait at the exit of the channel, determined to exert a supreme effort to take the fullest advantage of this golden opportunity, although these daring raiders knew that they would all be food for torpedoes and shells. Our I-model Submarine No. 44 was one of these doomed boats.

The capital ships maneuvered down the route with marvelous dexterity, moving in the darkness without any lights at all, turning west then south in a zigzag path as they progressed through the cleared channel. Would it be possible for the slow-moving submarines out front, with their limited visibility in the middle of the night, to accomplish anything against this skillfully maneuvered fleet? Also, only twelve Japanese submarines were staking out the island of Oahu. Because of these circumstances, only four or five American destroyers, advancing so closely together that their sides almost touched in the inky darkness, were able to successfully forge passage for the fleet.

USS *Portland* (CA-33), May 1934. *Portland* was a heavy cruiser designed to comply with the Washington Naval Treaty. *Naval Historical Center (NH 716)*

USS *Indianapolis* (CA-35) crewmen pose with a life preserver, ca. 1935. *Indianapolis* was a Portland-class cruiser with a crew that numbered between 950 and 1,200 seamen. *Naval Historical Center (NH 83939)*

SECTION 2: THE UNITED STATES FLEET

Look at the splendid battle array of the United States Fleet as it slices through the blue waves en route to the Western Pacific! At a point 800 miles west of Midway Island, the ten impressive new 10,000-ton, 8-inch-gun cruisers *Northampton*, *Chester*, *Louisville*, *Chicago*, *Augusta*, *Portland*, *Astoria*, *Indianapolis*, *New Orleans*, and *Minneapolis*, spaced at 20-mile intervals, formed a screen for the western advance. These cruisers, charging across a broad front of 200 miles with all eyes alert and seeking the whereabouts of any Japanese fleet intent upon surprise, were the antennae of the United States Fleet. However, the apprehension existed that if the eight 10,000-ton Japanese cruisers were to make a surprise attack on one part of the screen, there would not be sufficient time for the ships on the other flank to go to the assistance of the attacked ships. For this reason, the aircraft carrier *Ranger* was stationed on the right flank of the screen, the new carrier *Langley* on the other, and a number of reconnaissance planes were constantly kept in the air reconnoitering an additional 100 miles to the front.

USS *Detroit* (CL-8) crew, April 1935. *Detroit* was an Omaha-class light cruiser launched in 1922, mounted with eight 6-inch guns and manned by about thirty officers and 430 sailors. *Naval Historical Center (UA 56.05.01 Carol Martin collection)*

 Japanese War Fantasy

USS *Idaho* (BB-42) and USS *Texas* (BB-35) in battle line, 1930. *Idaho*'s four triple "14/50" (14-inch, .50-caliber) gun turrets are trained to starboard. *Naval Historical Center (NH 73834)*

Behind the screen of cruisers and planes, at a distance of 400 miles, was the famous "circle formation." The ten 7,500-ton, 6-inch-gun cruisers—*Omaha, Milwaukee, Cincinnati, Raleigh, Detroit, Richmond, Concord, Trenton, Marblehead,* and *Memphis,* and many destroyers, were stationed on the outer rim of this great circular formation at 10-mile intervals, moving westward. Within this great circle, toward the center, were the remaining four heavy cruisers, and behind them at 1,000 yards steamed the twelve capital ships in two columns. In the right column were a total of six ships comprising the 16-inch-gun battleships *Maryland, Colorado,* and *West Virginia,* and the 14-inch-gun ships *California, Tennessee,* and *Idaho,* while in the left column were another five 14-inch-gun ships—*Pennsylvania, Arizona, New Mexico, Mississippi,* and *New York,* and the 12-inch-gun battleship *Arkansas*. The pennant of Admiral Davis, the battle fleet commander, flew high from the rear mast of the flagship *Maryland*, which was the leading ship in the right column. The commander in chief of the United States Fleet, Admiral Gordon, flew his flag from the battleship *Texas*, which steamed on the right flank of the battle fleet. Around the circumference of this formation, a great number of destroyers were deployed, charged with reconnaissance duty and protecting the main body.

The great aircraft carriers *Lexington* and *Saratoga*, and the cruiser-carrier *Takoma* formed a separate squadron following behind the main body. Reconnaissance planes were constantly taking off from and returning to these three ships. The planes were engaged in searching out from the air any Japanese submarines that might be lying in wait in the path of the fleet's main body. It was a magnificent spectacle this great circular formation made when, at prearranged times, all the ships changed their courses and advanced over zigzag courses. The expertise with which these movements were carried out was the result of the constant training of the fleet in this formation during the ten years that had elapsed since the formation was first practiced in the great maneuvers of 1925. Truly, the synchronized movements of many units of the fleet bore out the meaning of the name "United States Fleet."

USS *Saratoga* landing aircraft, 1935. *Naval Historical Center (NH 80-g-651292)*

 Japanese War Fantasy

1925 Maneuvers
The "great maneuvers of 1925" refers to the US Navy exercise Fleet
Problem V conducted in March–April 1925, during which an aggressor
force with an aircraft carrier (USS *Langley*) simulated an attack on Hawaii.

United States
MID translator's note: In Japanese, the characters composing the name
"United States" may be read literally as "the harmonizing of the group."

"Under these circumstances, how would it be possible for Japanese submarines to even reach the fleet?" asked Admiral Gordon, as he looked with a satisfied air from the bridge of his flagship at the coordinated movements of his detachments.

"It is a fact, though, that there are Japanese submarines about," answered the flagship commander to the admiral. "The proof of what I say is the fact of the Japanese submarines that were unable to attack us at the time we were leaving Oahu . . ."

"Oh, don't worry about those," vaingloriously replied the admiral. "It was my suggestion that we scatter several hundred mines outside of Oahu harbor, and they neutralized those submarines very effectively."

Texas' captain remained silent but thought to himself, "This is another example of a commander who believes the maxim that 'The method to subjugate enemy submarines is to use an unlimited number of mines.'" The admiral's idea of the countermeasures to be employed against Japanese submarines was not to avoid them, but to take advantage of the great wealth of the United States to produce an unlimited quantity of mines and to use these lavishly against Japan's underwater craft. The captain of the flagship did not know how many mines the destroyers expected to lay, but he did know that the number of these devices that the destroyers could carry was very large. The captain had remained silent when the foolish order had been circulated to all capital ships, "All ships will carry 200 mines each for use by destroyers." Thus, the ships of this great fleet were loaded to capacity for their long journey and had been forced, for want of other storage space, to store the mines in the quarters of the crews in the middle decks. If, by accident, fire should break out in these quarters, the damage that would result would be far greater than any the Japanese submarines could possibly inflict.

However, the admiral left no doubt in anyone's mind as to his faith in mines. He expounded the creed to all and sundry without exception. "To subjugate Japanese submarines, you need only to throw in a large number of mines." Moreover, results so far had shown that there was a degree of truth in his words.

SECTION 3: JAPANESE GRAND IMPERIAL HEADQUARTERS

All was in confusion at the Japanese Grand Imperial Headquarters. Officers with general staff insignia dashed busily through the corridors with lips firmly set. Stern-faced sentinels stood stiffly erect at the entrances to conference rooms and challenged all persons in civilian garb who passed through the halls.

"Hey! Newspaper correspondents are not allowed to go there!"

In one conference room, the vice chief of the naval general staff, all navy department division chiefs, the chief of naval operations, and three army general staff officers gathered.

"First, read that wireless message," ordered Vice Admiral Matsukawa, the vice chief of the naval general staff.

"Very good!" responded the chief of naval operations (CNO) as he rose from his seat. He then read the following message:

"As of the 19th at 5:10 o'clock, at a point located north latitude 29 degrees 10 minutes, south longitude 116 degrees 20 minutes, ten enemy ships of the Omaha class in circle formation were discovered. Within the circle formation, the enemy strength is thirteen battleships, four deck class cruisers, and three aircraft carriers, *Lexington*, *Saratoga*, and one other. Behind the warships, eight troop-laden transports and supply ships were noted. Speed of fleet: 16 knots. At time of discovery, the course of the enemy fleet was west-southwest." The CNO continued, "This message was received from an air cruiser on distant reconnaissance in the Marshall Islands. Remember, this is the point where the enemy was located when the message was transmitted."

All eyes fixed on the point on the map where the CNO was pointing. It was just slightly south of the midpoint of a line between Hawaii and Yokosuka.

"Their course was west-southwest. Then, they are speeding toward the Philippines, are they not?" inquired an army officer in a low voice of a naval officer next to him.

"No. You are wrong. You see, the fleet moves on a zigzag course in order to escape submarines lying in wait for it, so we can never definitely state that the course of the enemy ships point, at any given time, to their actual objective. Furthermore, if you draw a line from the island of Oahu to the point where the fleet was discovered, and extend it westward, you can't fail to see that the fleet is bound for the Ogasawara Islands."

The army officer turned to the CNO and asked, "How many days would it take the enemy fleet to reach the Philippines?"

"I don't know. Perhaps two weeks . . ."

"Then it's no use," interjected one of the division chiefs. "Not only is it impossible to have the southern squadron return from Konko and Hona, but even if it was possible, we could not match our eight ships against their thirteen."

"What is the ratio of eight ships to thirteen?" asked the army officer who had first spoken. He picked up a pencil and started to calculate. "They are 60 percent superior. However, does it necessarily follow that they can win even if they are 60 percent superior?"

"Well, we hope that the submarines we sent after them from Hawaii to Midway Island will be able to narrow that 60 percent ratio," declared the division chief. "However, this is merely a mathematical conversation. In my opinion, the situation indicates that our submarines may fail to have any great effect, and I don't think that we can get a decision until our southern fleet returns. For the present, I think we should move our main fleet into the Inland Sea or some similar place and keep it from contact with the enemy for a little while."

"Are you advocating the doctrine of running away from the enemy?" snapped the vice chief of the naval general staff.

"I disagree with that Inland Sea plan," said the CNO. "If Japan avoids decisive action now, it is certain that the enemy will seize the Ogasawara Islands. We know that this will undoubtedly occur because we have just received a message stating that the enemy fleet is accompanied by transports bearing army troops. Furthermore, you are all familiar with the state of our defenses in the Ogasawara Islands."

"I don't like the plan," announced the vice chief of the naval general staff. "We must meet conditions as they exist. It is too soon yet to write off our submarines as a failure. We must resolve to bring on a decisive battle despite our 60 percent inferiority, and all arrangements must be made accordingly."

"Shall I notify at once the commander in chief of the Combined Fleet?" asked the CNO. "They have a fine opportunity right now."

"No, wait a moment," said the vice chief of staff. "The chief of naval general staff is coming in . . . The division chief who just advocated the Inland Sea plan appears to have more to say."

Admiral Osami Nagano (1880–1947), commander in chief of the Combined Fleet, ca. 1940. *Naval Historical Center (NH 63422)*

"I have always held a doubt as to the efficacy of the submarine. We can't expect these craft, with their slow submerged speed, to accomplish much. However, if we had 80,000 or 90,000 tons of submarines, perhaps opportunity for the use of some of them in battle might occur. But we are not so fortunate, for, as a result of the London Treaty, Japan was forced to reduce her submarine force to 52,000 tons."

"You're bringing up the London Treaty again?!?" laughed the CNO. "That treaty was made to preserve the peace in the future, but at a time such as this when we are faced with meeting the attack of a large enemy fleet, there is no use reviving the academic discussion as to whether it was just or not."

One hour after the conference ended, the CNO had obtained imperial sanction. He issued the momentous order to Admiral Nagano, commander in chief of the Combined Fleet. At naval general staff headquarters, all work subsided for a while, and the section chiefs, especially the CNO, caught their breath. However, the decision did not lighten the fears of the general staff. On the contrary, it added fresh uneasiness to an already uncertain situation in which the basic trouble was lack of exact information about what the enemy was contemplating.

"Do they think that our fleet will be able to defeat an enemy more than 60 percent stronger, simply because this unreasonable order has been given?!?"

Osami Nagano led a lengthy visit of Japanese naval cadets to the United States, during which he laid a wreath at the Tomb of the Unknown Soldier in Arlington National Cemetery, 1927. *Naval Historical Center (NH 96118)*

Admiral Osami Nagano

Admiral Osami Nagano was one of the Imperial Japanese Navy's leading visionaries and strategists before and during the Second World War. He excelled at the Japanese naval academy at the turn of the century, mastered English at Harvard University about 1915, and enjoyed duty as naval attaché at Japan's embassy in Washington in 1920. He oversaw a lengthy 1927 visit by Japanese naval cadets to the US, which afforded him opportunities to watch Babe Ruth play baseball, eat breakfast with President Coolidge, and lay a wreath at the Tomb of the Unknown Soldier in Arlington National Cemetery. He remained a staunch proponent of both a strong navy and peaceful solutions to the US-Japanese rivalry in the Pacific until the consensus among his younger, militant colleagues compelled him to accept the inevitability of war in 1941.

Japanese War Fantasy

CHAPTER 6
Initiative

SECTION 1: THE JAPANESE ADVANCE FLEET

The advance fleet steamed a short distance in front of the main fleet and contained the flower of Japan's navy: *Chokai*, *Maya*, *Atago*, *Takao*, *Ashigara*, *Haguro*, and *Myoko*. It reported that it had engaged a great enemy fleet of 10,000-ton cruisers 200 miles east of the Ogasawara Islands. Admiral Nagano, commander in chief of the Japanese fleet, ordered all detachments of the main fleet to increase their speed to 20 knots and proceed east at high speed. Upon receipt of a message from their reconnaissance planes confirming the location of the main enemy fleet, the Japanese fleet moved into battle formation and advanced to attack. Unfortunately, just as advance elements of both main fleets arrived within gunfire range, night fell. So, the engagement ended without any action except the firing of one or two ranging shots by two or three of the ships in order to bolster confidence. As the firing ceased, the thick darkness of the southern sea settled down quickly. Both fleets, planning a decisive action on the morrow, disappeared in the darkness.

Japanese cruiser *Chokai*, ca. 1932. *Naval Historical Center (NH 82080)*

Japanese cruiser *Maya*, forecastle and 8-inch guns, 1939. *Naval Historical Center (NH 73027)*

Japanese cruiser *Atago*, as modernized in 1939, depicted in ship recognition drawing prepared by US Office of Naval Intelligence. *Naval Historical Center (NH 97770)*

Japanese War Fantasy

Japanese cruiser *Atago* underway, 1934. *Naval Historical Center (NH 73022)*

Japanese cruiser *Ashigara* off Tsingtao, China, 1938. *Naval Historical Center (NH 78057)*

Japanese cruiser *Haguro* slicing through the wake of another IJN cruiser. In the foreground is a Type 89 127 mm/40 (5-inch) twin antiaircraft gun, the most common antiaircraft gun in the fleet. *Naval Historical Center (NH 73018)*

Japanese cruiser *Haguro*. *Naval Historical Center (NH 88373)*

 Japanese War Fantasy

Japanese cruiser *Myoko* off Yokosuka, 1934. *Naval Historical Center (NH 73020)*

Ogasawara Islands

The Ogasawara Islands were known to the US Navy as the Bonin Islands, an archipelago of about thirty islands about 600 miles south of Tokyo. They were sparsely populated and included the islands of Chichi Jima and Iwo Jima.

The destroyer *Kurumi* was one of the ships in the destroyer flotilla attached to the Japanese advance fleet. This was the second time that the *Kurumi* had been in battle with the enemy. After the voices of the guns had become silent, the ships had received no information as to where the enemy and the Japanese main fleets had withdrawn or where the decisive battle would be fought when day broke the next morning. There was only one thing that was certain, and that was that during the night before the action, the Japanese destroyer squadrons must exert every effort to find the enemy main fleet, which would be hidden by darkness, and strike into it. As a result of the failure of the Japanese submarines that had been stationed in various strategic locations in the Pacific, to interfere in any way whatsoever with the enemy fleet, the very important duty of reducing the strength of the enemy main fleet to assist the Japanese main fleet fell on the shoulders of the destroyer squadrons. It was imperative that this important duty be accomplished now, tonight, prior to the beginning of the engagement between the two main fleets in the morning. Tsuyoshi Kawano, the gunner of the rear torpedo tubes of the destroyer *Kurumi* had remained at his battle position since the engagement earlier in the day and was completely drenched by the salty water. This man, who thus waited for the next battle, had not even had time to get his food, and he must have been very hungry. Still, he showed no signs of wanting to change his wet clothing or to have something to eat. The ardor of battle seemed to have so intensified his spiritual self that he could suppress his physical needs.

Did the Japanese advance fleet acquit itself well in today's engagement? There are no words in the human vocabulary that will do justice to the bravery that the fleet displayed when it met the enemy. In truth, when the eight Japanese 10,000-ton cruisers struck the enemy fleet of ten cruisers of the same tonnage and two aircraft carriers, a bloody battle ensued in which the Japanese showed determination to sacrifice their lives to shell or sink the enemy craft rather than withdraw.

When the enemy's heavy cruiser squadron of ten ships had been first sighted on the eastern horizon, Kawano was not frightened. He remarked to himself, "We are two ships less than they, but we have a great deal more courage. We have been asleep in the Ogasawara Islands since yesterday morning, so our heads are clear, and we are itching for a fight."

Japanese cruiser *Kumano* was a Mogami-class ship designed around the restrictions of the Washington Naval Conference with 6.1-inch guns, 1939. *Naval Historical Center (NH 73028)*

Japanese cruiser *Suzuya*, like other Mogami-class ships, wielded five turrets of triple 6.1-inch guns and could attain a top speed of 35 knots. *Naval Historical Center (NH 73034)*

However, ten minutes later, the enemy heavy cruiser squadron was joined by two aircraft carriers, and Kawano's mindset shifted slightly. "Hey, that's a little dangerous now!"

Nevertheless, the commanding officer of the Japanese advance fleet ordered a dash straight for the aircraft carriers and thus started the battle at sunrise.

The result of the engagement, after two hours of fighting, was that the two enemy carriers, which had been the target objectives of the Japanese fleet, as well as two of the enemy cruisers, had been destroyed. But the price that the Japanese had had to pay for accomplishing this had been very great. When the big main fleets of both sides appeared on the horizon to the southeast and southwest, and the Japanese advance fleet withdrew in the direction of the Japanese main fleet, there were only two ships left out of the original eight that had composed the advance fleet two hours before!

"I believe that this naval battle was more terrible than anything that has ever been conceived up to the present time," said Kawano, recalling the terrible sights of an hour before. However, that bloody naval engagement was only the opening act in the drama which was yet to come. Of course, the night fighting which was to come for the destroyers was the particular duty of such craft, but the battle that was to follow the next morning would indeed be the great naval battle of the Pacific.

About one hour later, Kawano, standing on the lower deck of the destroyer, observed a great number of fire-like streaks stab into the sky from starboard. These presently merged into two searchlight beams that seemed to be searching for something as they panned from right to left. Suddenly, the two lights converged on some single point, and orange-colored sparks flecked the night's darkness. After a few seconds, Kawano thought he heard a roar of guns reverberating like distant thunder. Then, a bluish pillar of fire rose from the water and lit up the sea and sky in the direction of the enemy. A second later, the light extinguished, and everything returned to its former state of darkness and quiet.

"Oh my!" exclaimed a man poised by the torpedo tube. Just then, the quiet of the darkness was shattered by a scream. Someone then called out in a startled voice, "Who is that? Did I step on somebody's hand?"

"Be careful!" rasped a voice in the darkness. "There's somebody here!" The injured one murmured, "That hurt!" rubbing his hand. "Who are you anyway? Aren't you the doctor?"

"Oh, that's Kawano, isn't it?" remarked the man who had trod upon the other's hand. "It's so dark here I couldn't see. Forgive me."

"Still, I think that you'd better bandage the tip of my finger, doctor," replied Kawano.

"Ha!" laughed the surgeon. "In another hour, your whole arm might be shot off, so let's put off the medical treatment until then."

Torpedoman Kawano laughed roughly. "Is that so, doc?" he inquired. "Is the enemy already so close?"

The surgeon, a civilian officer, laughed. "I don't know where they are . . . I asked the captain just now, but he said that he didn't know whether those star shells we just saw were from our ships or the enemy's."

SECTION 2: TORPEDOMAN KAWANO

"Say, Tamura! Wake up! Wake up!" shouted Kawano a few hours later as he shook a seaman who was sleeping near the torpedo tube and snoring loudly. "Are you the kind of fellow who goes to sleep on post?"

The night had grown late, and young seamen, worn out from the day's work, had begun to surrender to sleep in ones and twos.

"Oh, was I asleep?" mumbled the low-ranking seaman in a carefree voice. "I guess I was just bushed."

"Stand up and let the breeze blow on you. Get wet if you feel drowsy."

The sailor, upset by the outrageous words of the torpedoman, made no reply. "Hey, Kawano," he asked, "What would you do in a case like this: suppose there were two girls—one very beautiful and the other fresh and unsophisticated but not good looking—who both wanted you very much. Which one would you choose?"

"Say, what kind of talk is that?" asked torpedoman Kawano, contemplatively. "I would need to have time to think that over before I could answer."

"No joking, it's the truth. Those two girls have fallen in love with me! I don't know what to do . . ."

"Are you still talking about your love affairs, Tamura? Let's change the subject. I'm sick of it."

"No, indeed. I just had a dream about them," said Tamura, laughing softy as he looked out into the darkness. "In my dream, I asked you to decide for me which one of the two I should choose."

Kawano, considering the subject to be foolish, did not reply. But true to his nature, Tamura continued to pursue the topic regardless of whether he had received an answer or not.

"Now, in regard to the pretty one, Kawano. She is surpassingly beautiful, I tell you. But wouldn't it be hard to be the hubby of such a beautiful girl? You might get tired of so much beauty continuously under your very nose. On the other hand, do you think that if I married her, I might forget the exquisite beauty of her face after she becomes my better half?"

"Shut up, that's not funny," scolded the gunner to the seaman. Then, once more wiping the wind-blown spray off the lenses of his binoculars, he put them to his eyes and noticed a strange light in the darkness.

"Oh!" said someone near the torpedo tube who also noticed the same strange light. "What is that flashing?"

"It's a signal. It's a special signal from one of our ships," said another man.

"Hmmmm . . . It's like the saying, 'The password of the river and the mountain,'" said Tamura. "How can we tell whether that is a signal from friend or enemy?"

There was no one on the ship, except those on the bridge, who could answer that question. However, all doubt was dispelled when a pale searchlight beam suddenly reflected in the water, followed by a burst of orange sparks that accompanied the firing of a gun.

Searchlight and bridge of Japanese cruiser *Aoba*, 1936. Powerful searchlights were vital for implementing the Japanese Navy's imperative for night-fighting superiority. *Naval Historical Center (NH 73015)*

"It's the enemy!" yelled torpedoman Kawano, opening the front port and peering out into the darkness. "There are two enemy ships!"

The two ships, discovered in the darkness to the front by Kawano, appeared to be big battleships and were in a single column steaming along together, while the Japanese destroyer flagship, *Kurumi*, was running on a course to the left of and parallel to the searchlight beam sent out by the light on the foremost enemy ship.

"Another shot!" said someone as again the orange sparks flew from the great black shape of the battleships.

When the distance between the ships became less, the noise of the enemy's gunfire became deafening. A rain of shots from the enemy ships began sweeping around a circular arc, while the beams from their

Japanese War Fantasy

US sailor operating a searchlight, ca. 1930s. Searchlight technology was a naval priority before radar revolutionized surface surveillance. *Naval Historical Center (NH 124097)*

searchlights highlighted objectives like pointing fingers. Simultaneously with each broadside, countless columns of water sprang up over the surface of the sea like fountains.

And *Kurumi*? It was the leading ship of a three-ship column, and every time the pale red flashes lit up the scene, the noise of the terrific gunfire was borne to the ship by the wind blowing from the front. What was that? Had the leading enemy ship, which was drawing the gunfire from all directions, just exploded and disintegrated?

At the torpedo tube of the destroyer *Kurumi*, Kawano unconsciously staggered as the ship moved sharply under a change of rudder. Every time the rudder changed, the speed of the engines increased, which caused the torpedo tubes to rattle and shake violently. Although the officers on the bridge did not know what was happening, the strange actions of the destroyer were evidence of Lieutenant Maki's determination to cut his ship out of column, even though it would involve his going far from his ordered position, and to proceed independently to try heroically to torpedo the enemy ships.

Lieutenant Maki depicted on *Kurumi*'s bridge. Illustration by Katsuichi Kabashima in *Nichibeisen Miraiki*. University of Maryland Prange collection

Up to this time, none of the enemy's shots had fallen near the destroyer *Kurumi*.

"Say, are these ships the Japanese aircraft carriers *Kaga* and *Akagi*?" shouted a *Kurumi* seaman, addressing his fellows and pointing to the two large enemy ships now visible on the starboard and moving on a course parallel to the destroyer. This man had seemingly gone crazy as the destroyer chased after the enemy.

"Why don't they stop firing?" he shrieked frantically. "Can't they see that they are shooting at their own ships?!?"

"Be quiet, Tamura!" hissed Kawano, scolding the hysterical man. Kawano then calmly looked through the aiming device of the torpedo tube, impatiently awaiting orders from the bridge to fire.

However, the officers on the bridge did not know whether to fire or not because the enemy ships were constantly changing their positions. Presently, the second of the two enemy ships came into the line of fire, and, although it presented a fine target for a brief moment, not a torpedo was discharged at her from *Kurumi*.

No one on the bridge had pressed the telegraph signal to fire, had they?

Was it possible that what Tamura said could be true? Were these two great ships, steaming right past the destroyer, really our own Japanese aircraft carriers?

Japanese destroyer *Mikazuki,* a Mutsuki-class vessel launched in 1927, under bombardment, ca. 1943. *Naval Historical Center (NH 83013)*

Destroyer *Kurumi*
dodging enemy
shells. Illustration
by Katsuichi
Kabashima in
*Nichibei-sen
Miraiki. University
of Maryland Prange
collection*

SECTION 3: DESTROYER *KURUMI*

The next moment, the second of the two enemy ships picked out the *Kurumi* in the ghostly beam of its many-candlepower searchlight. Immediately, the Japanese destroyer became the center of the water columns that suddenly sprouted into the air. The noise of exploding shells reverberated in the ears, and a metallic din arose as shell fragments whistled through the air and struck the walls, masts, and stacks of the destroyer.

"Who in the devil was the fellow who did that!" howled a man behind the torpedo tubes as he fell backward to the deck with a thud. Kawano, who was busy with the aiming mechanism of the torpedo firing tube, had no time to pay any attention to either his own safety or the fallen sailor. Leaning against the right side of the torpedo tube, Kawano was watching the enemy ship with his neck outstretched like a crane. The strange ships, if judged by their appearance along the line of the upper deck, did in fact resemble Japanese aircraft carriers, as Tamura had said. But, looking up at the towering sides of the carriers in the ashy light of the ghostly searchlight, surprisingly wide smokestacks could be seen jutting high into the air like mountains.

"I am positive that they are enemy aircraft carriers."

Japanese aircraft carrier *Kaga*, easily identifiable with low-profile stacks, 1936. *Naval Historical Center (NH 73060)*

Japanese aircraft carrier *Akagi*, 1941. *Naval Historical Center (NH 73059)*

Among Japan's aircraft carriers, *Kaga*, *Akagi*, *Hosho*, *Ryujo*, and *Banryu*, there was not one with stacks rising high above the deck. God be praised! God be praised that there could not be the least doubt that the ships before their eyes were enemy ships!

Nevertheless, even then the officers on the bridge of *Kurumi* took no action. What were they thinking? To refrain from combat when it was perfectly clear that these ships were enemy ships? Didn't they realize that this God-given opportunity would be lost forever in mere seconds?

It was a time for action. It was no time for idleness.

The black shapes of the two great enemy ships were clearly discernible through the smoke of cannon fire and water spray from falling shells. The aiming mechanism of the Japanese destroyer was resolved with a clanking noise to point to the foremost of the two ships. The gunner waited with bated breath for the order to fire. At this moment, torpedoman Kawano thought that he heard something strike the torpedo tubes with a noise like a hammer striking a steel plate, and at the same time he felt something strike his body. Then, suddenly he felt a fiery pain in his right side, and he became conscious of something warm flowing from his body. He cried out, "Oh!" involuntarily, gritted his teeth, and kept his eye trained as before in the aiming mechanism of the torpedo tubes.

Presently, the leading ship of the enemy squadron entered the field of sight of the aiming apparatus. Kawano bent forward slightly, fumbled around with his left hand for one of the triggers, found it, and swiftly exerted his entire strength to pull it. With a whoosh like a fast express train rushing through a tunnel, a bright silver fish, 25 inches in diameter, flew out of the torpedo tube. *Kurumi* had thus set loose upon the enemy an engine of destruction that nothing on earth could now recall. In the midst of the din of guns firing and shells splashing, a loud hissing sound of escaping steam from the enemy ship pierced through the noise. Then, a great cloud of white steam billowed out of the carrier's forepart. Next, in a brief space of time, the loud pulsations of her principal engines stopped abruptly.

"Her boilers are broken! She can't move," muttered Kawano, feeling as if everything under the sun was finished. The roaring gunfire from the enemy ship ceased.

Shortly, the steam stopped howling from the escaping ship, and a red pillar of fire arose into the sky in its place. A deluge of water was pouring into the ship like a waterfall. A brief second later, when the water subdued the towering flames, another more terrible red and orange glare appeared.

Destroyers laying a smokescreen, 1936. *Naval Historical Center (NH 109940)*

The Japanese destroyer crew watched breathlessly as this new fire grew. Then, suddenly, in a burst of smoke, sparks, and flame, the torpedoed ship's masts, stacks, airplanes, and an unfathomable amount of torn and destroyed weapons and structural parts were blown high into the sky.

"The fire reached her magazines!" yelled Kawano.

The stricken ship suddenly stood on end in the sea with her nose pointed down and then plunged headfirst to the bottom of the ocean.

At this time, the beam from the searchlight of the second enemy ship struck full in torpedoman Kawano's eyes as the shell-torn destroyer attempted again to leave this scene of terrible carnage. Suddenly, another destroyer appeared in the searchlight beam and sped to starboard with sparks belching from its stacks. Behind the newly arrived destroyer billowed a thick black smokescreen, and the enemy ship disappeared from sight.

Torpedoman Kawano stood listlessly by the torpedo tube. He felt a numbness stealing over the right side of his body. He warily touched at his lower right side with his left hand. "Blood!" he exclaimed, as he looked at his blood-stained hand and noticed for the first time that he had been hurt. "I have been wounded," he thought to himself. However, it was certainly a strange thing that he felt not the slightest pain. In fact, he did not feel as much pain as he would have had he struck his finger with a hammer.

When he started to speak, he received a great shock. He looked around to find somebody to talk with. He noticed only three or four men lying dead on the steel deck. He could not see a single soul alive.

How was this? Had everybody been killed by the enemy fire? Was there not even one survivor of all who had stood around the aft torpedo tubes?

"Tamura, oh, Tamura," called Kawano.

No one answered his call.

Kawano stumbled to the forward part of *Kurumi*, which was shrouded in darkness. He reached the entrance to the mess hall and collided with someone. Kawano inquired, "Is the captain safe? Is Lieutenant Maki safe?"

"Captain?" replied a voice that sounded like that of the surgeon. "Why, the captain and all the officers on the bridge were killed."

CHAPTER 1

Battle to Decide Air Superiority

SECTION 1: NAGANO

The electric light on the table etched Admiral Nagano's face in profile as he studied a chart. His luxuriant hair framed a broad forehead that bespoke wisdom; the light of keen intelligence glimmered in his eyes, and his firm jaw and broad mouth projected great determination.

US Navy Grumman FF-1 fighters (Squadron VF-5). The FF-1 was the first carrier aircraft with retractable landing gear and was the workhorse of naval aviation throughout the 1930s. *Naval Historical Center (NH 83927)*

US Navy Grumman FF-1 fighter landing on USS *Lexington*, February 1933. *Naval Historical Center (NH 51373)*

"By the way," said Nagano, the commander in chief, raising his head to address the chief of staff. "What is the ratio of the air strength of the enemy and our fleets?"

"In combat planes, the enemy has fifty-four machines each aboard both *Saratoga* and *Lexington* and eighteen on the cruiser-carrier *Takoma*, making a total of 126 planes. To oppose these, we have about 105 fighting planes aboard the ships of this fleet," replied the chief of staff from his great store of knowledge. He then continued, "Furthermore, if we add the forty-five planes in the aviation units at Chichi Jima in the Ogasawara Islands, we will have a total of 150 machines."

USS *Takoma*
When Fukunaga wrote the novelette in 1933, there were only three existing US aircraft carriers: *Langley* (CV-1), *Lexington* (CV-2), and *Saratoga* (CV-3). Author Fukunaga christened the next carrier-to-be *Tacoma*. However, CV-4 was christened USS *Ranger* when launched in 1934.

Chichi Jima seaplane base and town under attack, September 2, 1944. *Naval Historical Center (80-G-248844)*

Chichi Jima
Chichi Jima is the largest island in the Ogasawara Archipelago, a formation of rocky outcrops draped with tropical flora jutting out of the Pacific Ocean 600 miles off the Japanese coast. A small base of the Imperial Japanese Navy was established on Chichi Jima in 1914 and eventually hosted long-range radio stations, an air base, and other military units.

"Keep the machines in the Ogasawara Islands separate for a while. Do you think that we have a reasonable prospect of victory with 105 planes?" Nagano asked the aviation general staff officer.

"I believe that we can count on winning," answered the aviation officer stiffly. "Since the loss of the *Ranger* and the *Langley*, we are only twenty planes inferior to the enemy."

Japanese War Fantasy

Japanese battleship *Mutsu*, ca. 1938. *Naval Historical Center (NH 111591)*
Center (80-G-248844)

"If we do not take advantage of this opportunity tonight," said the chief of staff, "the Japanese fleet will never live to tell the tale."

"Very well," the commander in chief said, rising and making the decision. "Proceed with the plan as quickly as possible."

"Very well, sir. Slightly before daybreak, at about 4:30 a.m., we will begin the attack."

"Two hours from now!" said the commander in chief, taking out an old-fashioned pocket watch and looking at it. "Well, I'm going to catch forty winks. Please wake me at the proper time." Nagano headed down to the officers' lounge for a nap.

In the quiet of the chart room, the chief of staff assembled a half-dozen officers. Throughout the night, they worked out the strategy and plans to be employed at daybreak.

The consensus of the general staff officers was that there could be no doubt of victory if, tonight, the Japanese fleet would approach as close as possible to the main fleet of the enemy and then, at daybreak, promptly open the action by a large-scale attack against the enemy's air strength.

"How about it?" asked the chief of staff, glancing around. "Well, please wake me when you call the commander in chief. You all better try to get a little sleep, too."

"Not me. Before battle, one should enjoy himself. I am just the opposite from the commander in chief," remarked one general staff officer, scratching his head.

"Well, let's go up to the bridge and cool our heels a bit," said a general staff commander. The two left the chart room.

Japanese battleship *Mutsu*, ca. 1932. *Naval Historical Center (NH 111588)*

On the bridge, they found the ship's captain, his second-in-command (the executive officer), the navigator, and the ship's brain trust gathered around the compass, speaking occasionally in low tones and glancing out over the dark sea. Looking down, about 100 meters in front, the bow of the ship could be seen now and then lazily disappearing under foaming waves. Slightly closer, sprayed by waves pelting the bow, squatted two gun turrets, each with a pair of massive 40-centimeter (16-inch) guns thrusting out of the sides. Looking toward the stern, the big smokestacks loomed up, shaped like potato bugs. Far away, the blank bulk of the second ship, *Nagato*, could be seen following along in the rear at 1,000 meters distance.

 Japanese War Fantasy

Japanese battleship *Nagato*, foremast and 16-inch guns, 1938. *Naval Historical Center (NH 111611)*

"They're still at it, ain't they?" remarked the executive officer (the "XO") to the general staff officer as a thunderous sound echoed in the distance. "How many of the enemy do you think we will be able to account for in this night's battle?"

"I once saw that clumsy enemy make an attack with a torpedo boat squadron, and I felt very sorry for them. So, if we do not hear good news from our fleet as a result of this night's fight, I will certainly be very much surprised," said the general staff officer. "Nevertheless, we will not have an easy time with their capital ships after day breaks."

"When day breaks?!?" asked the XO in a surprised voice, looking at the luminous dial of his wristwatch. "Why, that is only two hours from now! Shall we go now and make an inspection of the ship?"

The general staff officer declined the invitation, but the XO left the cool bridge to begin his inspection of the hot, steamy interior of the ship. It was a tiresome duty, but it was the duty prescribed for the XO as second in command. Making the ship ready for battle demanded the XO's attention to an exhausting list of tedious details: confirming that all water-tight doors were securely closed; that station lights were all in order; that reserve lights were positioned properly; that the firefighting squad had been designated; and that fire hoses were prepared for immediate use. In addition, the XO's duties included trying out each fire pump at least once, checking that sufficient gas masks were available, etc.

Descending a number of ladders, the XO first visited the 14-centimeter (5.5-inch) gun battery. This secondary gun battery was pitch-black dark for fear of light being visible outside the ship. The young officer in charge stood stiffly at attention when he saw the XO approach. The battery commander saluted the XO and barked, "Nothing to report in the forward gun battery!"

The XO inspected the guns, the gun carriages, the ammunition, and the breech blocks, nodding silently with satisfaction.

"Executive officer, is there any news about the enemy situation?" inquired the young officer. "The only news we've heard is simply that we might expect a night attack. Can you tell me anything further? Everybody has been waiting impatiently since early evening to get into action."

"Don't worry!" replied the XO with a laugh. "At daybreak you will have plenty of opportunity to do some fighting."

The battery commander laughed happily and said, "Thank you very much, sir."

From this battery, the XO walked on, opened a steel door, and stepped through it into the next compartment. "These are fine fellows," he thought to himself as he looked over the gun crew of the next battery. "Do your duty at the proper time, men!"

The XO proceeded from one dark compartment to another and from one battery to another until he had made the complete round of his inspection. At the guns, the necessary ammunition was positioned and ready. However, the members of the firefighting squads—officers, NCOs, and seamen—were all lamenting their fate because they were detailed for firefighting and were equipped with neither "rifles nor even bows and arrows!"

Nevertheless, the morale of the men on the upper decks was very high. This was not strange because, even though they were forced to work in very narrow and close quarters, they could see the enemy and take part in the fight. For this reason, the men on the upper decks considered themselves comparatively the luckiest on-board the ship.

The men in the places to which the XO descended next were not as fortunate. Shut in below the water line, in places resembling steel huts that had to be lit day and night by electric lights, these men labored in ignorance of what was happening to the ship—no matter which kind of battle might engage the vessel, they heard not the slightest sound of the loud concussions of the guns of their own ship nor the explosions of the enemy's shells when they found their mark. In the final analysis, however, they must be greatly respected, for, compared with the men above decks, these moles of the ship's bowels were not a whit less faithful and zealous. The XO did not neglect to let these powerfully muscled men, who labored in the ship's dismal depths, see from his expression that he was deeply sympathetic.

The XO again ascended a ladder and passed along the side of a gloomy-looking compartment where an electric light glimmered in the ceiling, illuminating glass bottles on wall shelves and rolls of bandages arranged in the closets. The white-robed doctors standing in front of the empty operating room bowed to him as he came up. "Will it begin soon?" asked the noncombatant chief surgeon, who was hungry for the fight to start and supply him with patients on whom to operate. His eyes lighting up, he continued, "My arm is just itching to do some carving!"

"Oh, I guess it will be an hour yet before it starts," replied the XO. "It'll be a little while yet," he repeated. After going through the battle medical dressing station, he ascended and descended countless more ladders. He inspected everything in the minutest detail, from powder magazines to torpedo tubes. Everywhere he went, the sailors immediately became thrilled, though they had not yet seen any enemy.

Finally, the XO visited the central control room in the heart of the ship, below the water line. Here, electric cables and speaking tubes that connected every part of the ship converged, and the room resembled a telephone exchange. An officer seated at a small desk in the center of the room appeared to be rehearsing the many commands and messages that would be handled once firing commenced. The officer would dispatch these commands via a messenger at his side to the various electrical transmitters in the room, where they would be flashed to every corner of the ship, from the gun batteries to the crow's nest.

"Everything is satisfactory," reported the central control room chief to the XO. "Even though we are inferior in numbers of guns, we will defeat the Yankees by our rate of fire."

"In the final analysis, it is the guns that count," declared the XO, who had formerly been chief gunnery officer, in encouraging the young control room chief. "Everything will be all right if we can repeat the record we made at last year's battle-firing practice."

SECTION 2: TWO KNOTS

The naval commander (general staff) read aloud the following message, which had just been delivered by the compressed air tube from the battle station wireless room:

"Message from reconnaissance plane of the carrier *Akagi*: thirteen enemy battleships located at point 553. Course northwest, moving in single column. Two ships, one apparently the carrier *Saratoga*, and the cruiser-carrier *Takoma* attached. Fourteen cruisers 10 miles to the west of this column. Course north-northwest, moving in two columns, stop."

A general staff lieutenant commander quickly plotted the enemy positions on the chart and reported to both the commander in chief and the chief of staff, "They are located here. The main enemy position is 13 miles north of our position."

"By heavens!" exclaimed the air officer, snatching the message from the hand of the general staff commander. "This means that during the night the enemy has lost one big aircraft carrier, and that the enemy planes are now reduced to seventy-two machines, which gives us, with our 105 planes, unquestioned superiority in the air."

"I did not know that our destroyer squadron had accomplished such a fine piece of work," said Admiral Nagano joyfully. "This destruction of one enemy carrier will be far and away of more service to us than would have been the sinking of one or two battleships."

"Sir!" The chief of staff addressed the commander in chief. "Under the changed conditions, shall we carry out our prearranged plan against the one remaining carrier?"

The commander in chief nodded his powerful head, whereupon the chief of staff spiritedly issued the following order: "Aviation general staff officer, take the first and second air squadrons at full strength and immediately attack the remaining enemy aircraft carrier and the *Takoma*! Now, captain . . ." he continued, turning to the flagship commander, "Course northwest, speed 20 knots."

The wind had died down, but the swells were very high. As the flagship *Mutsu* made a wide turn to the left, the commander in chief turned his binoculars on the other ships in the column. Even the enormous 33,000-ton *Nagato* was rising and falling in the large swells. Facing the east, where day was just beginning to break, the dull golden light reflected from the chrysanthemum shield on the prow of the ship. The shield came into and out of view with the rise and fall of the sea, which even exposed the red-black hull below the ship's waterline momentarily while water she had scooped up poured in a deluge from her two anchor ports. *Hyuga*, separated from *Nagato* by 1,000 meters, was followed at similar intervals by *Ise*, *Kirishima*, *Hiyei*, *Yamashiro*, and *Fuso*, steaming along like a long snake.

Japanese battleships *Nagato, Kirishima, Ise, Hyuga. Naval Historical Center (NH 111609)*

At a distance of 5,000 meters to the right of the Japanese main fleet, the five ships comprising the first and second Japanese aircraft carrier squadrons, *Akagi, Kaga, Ryujo, Hosho,* and *Banryu,* steamed along in column. However, when the signal was flashed from the flagship, all these ships simultaneously swung their bows into the wind and moved out. From the narrow decks of all the carriers, first one and then another plane took to the air, forming squadrons of nine planes each. When these squadrons totaled 150 planes, they pointed the noses of their machines to the east.

Japanese Aircraft Carrier *Banryu*
No aircraft carrier named *Banryu* ever existed. She roughly corresponds to the real-life *Hiryu,* which was launched in 1937 and supported the 1940 invasion of French Indochina, attacked Pearl Harbor in 1941 and Wake Island in 1942, and was sunk during the Battle of Midway in 1942.

Japanese aircraft carrier *Hosho*, October 1945. *Hosho* was the world's first ship designed as an aircraft carrier when launched in 1921, and she provided distant fleet support for operations against Pearl Harbor and Midway Island twenty years later. *Naval Historical Center (80-G-351904)*

"Even if we lose one plane for every one of the planes of the enemy when we destroy them, we will still have fifty machines left," said the chief of staff confidently as he watched the great air armada wing out of sight like a swarm of locusts. "No matter what happens, we will have control of the air!"

Japanese aircraft carrier *Hiryu*, April 1939. She corresponds to the fictional *Banryu* in Fukunaga's war story. *Naval Historical Center (NH 73063)*

 Japanese War Fantasy

Japanese Mitsubishi B2M Type 89, Nakajima A2N Type 90, and Aichi D1A1 Type 94 prepare to take off from carrier *Kaga*, May 1937. *Wikimedia Commons*

Just at this moment, the aviation general staff officer appeared from below and read aloud a message: "Wireless from Chichi Jima: forty-five battle planes and eighteen heavy bombers have just taken off for point 553."

Sixty-three Japanese planes from the Ogasawara Islands were in route to reinforce the 150 machines of the fleet. There was now not the slightest doubt of Japanese victory in the forthcoming air battle.

"We have overpowering superiority," joyfully exclaimed the commander in chief. "I imagine that even Admiral Gordon will now realize the great disadvantage of doing battle so far away from his base."

At this time, enemy planes, seemingly reconnaissance machines, flew one by one at high altitude over the Japanese fleet and then turned back toward their mother ships. Unquestionably, these enemy planes had been sent out to obtain information on the organization, course, and formation of the Japanese fleet. But the Japanese did not have time now to attack these individual planes.

Japanese reconnaissance planes were also maneuvering to the front and were reporting moment-by-moment by radio to the flagship about the enemy situation. As these messages were received, the general staff lieutenant commander plotted on the chart each position and formation of the Japanese and enemy forces and showed these to the commander in chief and the chief of staff. At 5:10 a.m., as the clouds shrouding the eastern horizon blazed red with the coming dawn, the Japanese officers grew tense as the sound of gunfire reached them from the direction into which their air squadrons had disappeared.

USS *Colorado* (BB-45) stern catapults and Vought O3U reconnaissance aircraft, ca. 1936. *Naval Historical Center (NH 107586)*

"The cruiser squadrons have opened fire!" announced the general staff lieutenant commander. "The sound is 39,000 meters away, and the leading ship of the main enemy fleet is 39,000 meters away."

The chief of staff had planned to open fire when the Japanese fleet reached a distance of 30,000 meters (16 sea miles) from the enemy. However, although the range at this time was slightly greater than anticipated, he ordered the battle pennants broken out from the main masts of all ships of his fleet. A moment after he gave this order, a series of air-splitting shots was heard, spaced two or three seconds apart, and then ten columns of water, each seemingly vying with the others for height, rose from the surface of the sea 1,000 meters to the starboard of the Japanese flagship *Mutsu*.

"By Jove!" exclaimed the chief of staff. "Turn all ships six points to port!"

Mutsu, *Nagato*, and the other six Japanese battleships simultaneously swung around on their rudders and tried to escape quickly to the left from the terrible concentration of fire.

The second salvo from the invisible enemy now whined through the air and fell a short 400 meters behind and to the starboard of the fleeing

Japanese cruiser formation, 1938. *Naval Historical Center (NH 73037)*

Japanese flagship. The sea, in an area of about 300 meters diameter, became a boiling hell of high columns of water rising one after the other with each enemy shot.

"It would be fatal to rush into that area," remarked the chief of staff with a serious face. "We can't help ourselves in this case because the enemy has three ships with 40-centimeter guns."

"It is a surprise to me, chief of staff," said the gunnery officer, grinding his teeth. "In truth, it is a surprise that the enemy's 40-centimeter guns can reach 39,000 yards."

39,000 yards is exactly 21 sea miles. This long 21-mile range of the enemy guns was immensely superior to the range of any guns in the Japanese fleet. Probably, the explanation for this was that the Americans had secretly increased the angle of elevation of their 40-centimeter (16-inch) guns by 40 or 50 degrees at the time of their great battleship modernization program two years ago, which was carried out with funds appropriated for industrial recovery in the United States.

However, notwithstanding their great guns, the enemy ceased firing after three trial salvos, probably because the Japanese main fleet, utilizing its 2-knot superiority in speed, had passed to the west beyond the range of the American guns. The 23-knot speed of the Japanese fleet, compared with the 21 knots of the enemy battleship squadrons, made the Japanese vessels an elusive foe.

Now what advantage would the Japanese make of their superior speed? It is certain that it was not for the purpose of running away and hiding that the Japanese fleet had come all the way to the east from the Ogasawara Islands. There is no doubt about it—Admiral Nagano had led his fleet of some 110 warships to this area with the determination to fight a decisive engagement, either with the fleet as a single unit or in detachments.

If this was so, what was the reason for the *Mutsu* and the other seven ships of the main Japanese fleet moving out of range to the westward in ladder formation as they were doing now? Is it not true that to say the fleet was "moving out of range" was really the same thing as saying that it was "running away?"

If the Japanese ships were to close in and shorten the range, they would meet a terrible fate without being able to fire a shot. They would be unable either to inflict any damage or to sink any enemy ships. It seemed that the commanders of the Japanese fleet were certainly faced with an extreme predicament as to what course to take! What was the best thing for them to do under the circumstances?

Admiral Nagano was utterly indifferent to these worries. Although all his officers, from the usually competent chief of staff down, were nonplussed by these adverse circumstances, the admiral disregarded them entirely. Pulling out his old-fashioned watch and glancing at it, he remarked in a calm and dignified manner, "What's this? It's just beyond daybreak and we still have between ten and fifteen hours left for fighting. Why don't you hurry? You haven't done a thing yet."

Now, to tell the truth, both the chief of staff and his assistant, like the commander in chief, appeared to be unworried and nonchalant. They impressed one as being of the firm conviction that, somehow or the other, the adverse situation of the Japanese fleet would soon undergo a dramatic change.

The most important factor that would determine whether the general situation would undergo a change was whether or not the Japanese fleet could obtain control of the air.

SECTION 3: CARRIER WAR

As was expected, the air battle ended in an overwhelming victory for the Japanese air forces.

Of course, it goes without saying that the officers of the United States air forces were not unskillful nor timid. Their fighting morale was as excellent as that of their Japanese antagonists. Their technique was as good as that possessed by any other airmen in the world. There were numerous Rickenbackers, Foncks, and von Richtofens in the United States naval aviation service. The fact that the American fleet had brought with them many superior Boeing and Curtiss planes made them doubly worthy foes. However, compared with the Japanese naval aviation service, they were not one whit better. Furthermore, the number of planes available to them at the scene of the battle was not equal to the number possessed by the Japanese.

"Rickenbackers, Foncks, and von Richtofens"
Fukunaga refers to World War I aces Eddie Rickenbacker of the US, René Paul Fonck of France, and Manfred von Richtofen of Germany.

Grumman F3F fighters were the mainstay of the US carrier fleet in the late 1930s. Corpus Christi, Texas, 1942. *Library of Congress (LC-USE6-D-007071)*

There are probably those who will retort, "Did you say that there was a shortage of planes in the American navy? Do you mean to seriously make such a foolish assertion?!?" The statement does seem open to question, but it is the truth, so there is no use talking about it. As further substantiation of this, the following remarks of Commander Burnett, chief of staff of the air service of the United States fleet, clearly bear out the truth of these assertions. Burnett was, with others, taken prisoner and made the following statement to his Japanese counterpart:

USS *Lexington* (CV-2) underway, March 1932. *National Archives (80-G-63333)*

"At the beginning of the war, we started immediately to convert five splendid passenger liners into aircraft carrier supply ships, but the reconstruction work on them was only half finished when the fleet started on this expedition, so we could not bring them along. For this reason, the United States fleet brought with it to the Western Pacific only *Saratoga* (33,000 tons), *Lexington* (33,000 tons), *Ranger* (13,800 tons), the new *Langley* (13,800 tons), and the cruiser-carrier *Takoma* (10,000 tons), making a total five-ship, aircraft carrier combined tonnage of 103,600 tons. Then, not only were *Ranger* and *Langley* sunk on the day prior to this battle in the desperate attack of the Japanese heavy cruisers, but on the following night the *Lexington* was also lost. It was impossible for us to keep control of the air with only two carriers, *Saratoga* and *Takoma*, which mounted a total of only seventy machines on both ships. We crossed swords with more than one hundred battle planes from the five Japanese aircraft carriers. Yes, it was an impossibility!"

USS *Ranger* (CV-4) aviators wearing cold-weather gear pose in front of a Grumman F3F fighter, February 1936. *National Archives (80-CF-8005-3)*

USS *Saratoga* (CV-3) crowded flight deck about to launch aircraft, May 1934. *National Archives (80-G-1027066)*

USS *Saratoga* (CV-3) flight deck viewed from the stern, showing arresting gear and dual 5-inch guns aft of her island, April 1936. The flight deck was 866 feet long. *Naval Historical Center (NH 51834)*

USS *Saratoga* (CV-3) aviators of Fighter Squadron 6 (VF-6) pose in front of a Boeing F4B fighter, Naval Air Station Hampton Roads, Virginia, August 1934. *National Archives (80-G-451350)*

Japanese War Fantasy

Nakajima B5N1 "Kate" bombers (IJN Type 97 model 11), Japan,1939. *National Archives (80-G-15399)*

Nakajima B5N1 "Kate" bomber (IJN Type 97), Naval Air Station Patuxent River, Maryland, 1943. The B5N first took flight in 1937 and was a mainstay of Japanese naval aviation throughout the war. *National Archives (80-G-427153)*

"When the Japanese planes came, nearly fifty Japanese bombers made a furious attack on the *Takoma* and *Saratoga*. The two ships put up a fine defense. People tell me that the remaining battle planes and antiaircraft guns of our ships brought down at least twenty Japanese machines. However, how could we defend ourselves successfully when determined Japanese bombers came at us from all sides, raining their bombs down upon our decks? Twenty minutes after the start of the battle, *Takoma* raised her stern to the sky and plunged headfirst into the sea. *Saratoga*, her deck shot full of holes, could not launch any more planes, and, of course, no more planes could land on her deck, either. Thus, our sea-landing fields vanished entirely, and our deck-landing planes that were circling around in the air were left to their own devices and were finally swallowed up by the sea. In this manner, the naval air service of the United States fleet was completely wiped out.

IJN "Kate" bomber shot down by USS *Lexington* near Eniwetok, December 1943. *Naval Historical Center (S-487.15)*

"On the Japanese side, their aircraft carriers were to a large extent destroyed, too. *Banryu* was sunk by the concentrated fire of the American cruisers. The flying deck of *Akagi* was destroyed, too, I remember. However, Japan's strong point was that she still had three aircraft carriers left. In a case such as this, there is a great difference between the side that has no aircraft carrier at all and the side that has three, two, or even only one of such ships. It was not only this factor, however, that determined the outcome. Another thing was the additional planes that reinforced the Japanese side. When the report reached us that the battle planes from the vicinity of the Ogasawara Islands [Bonins] had arrived and landed on the three carriers for refueling, we were convinced that the fight was hopeless. Our observation planes, equipped with pontoons for landing on water, were, for the most part, still in the air when your reinforcing planes arrived from the Ogasawara Islands. These newly arrived planes were responsible for driving our reconnaissance planes from the air until not even one plane remained. It was in this way that the planes with the rising sun on their wings gained complete control of the sky on the field of battle."

 Japanese War Fantasy

Above: Vought O3U-1 Corsair reconnaissance plane takes off from USS *Ranger* (CV-4), June 1934. *Naval Historical Center (NH 51872)*
Below: Vought O3U Corsair of USS *Augusta* aviation unit, Philippine Islands, ca. 1936. *Naval Historical Center (NH 78016)*

Vought O3U-3 Corsair (*left*) and Grumman J2F-1 (*right background*) reconnaissance planes on USS *Yorktown*, November 1937. *National Archves (80-CF-54862-2)*

Grumman J2F "Duck" reconnaissance plane from USS *Heron* aviation unit, Philippine Islands, 1936. *Naval Historical Center (NH 78018)*

SECTION 4: VICTORY

"Reconnaissance planes for observation of fire." These were the most important targets for which the commander in chief of the Japanese fleet was on the lookout, even though the battlefield had been swept so clean of enemy planes of this type that not even one remained. Ever since yesterday, when the attack on these enemy planes and the so-called sacrifice of the enemy carriers had resulted in victory in the air for the Japanese forces, the enemy fleet had been effectively blinded. This was the real reason for the destruction of the enemy aircraft.

The enemy had been blinded as a result of the battle for control of the air. This had been, in truth, the trump card in the strategy of the "60 percent navy."

The 60% Navy
The "60 percent navy" refers to ratios in naval construction tonnage set by the 1922 Washington Naval Treaty (and reiterated by the 1930 London Naval Treaty) at 5:5:3 (or 10:10:6) for the United States, Great Britain, and Japan.

The eastern sky had been cleaned up and put in order. Admiral Nagano came up to the bridge after finishing his breakfast, where the chief of staff addressed him. "Commander in chief, it is time to close in on the enemy. Look! You can't see a single reconnaissance plane over any of the ships!"

The earlier bombardment by the Americans' 40-centimeter (16-inch) guns from a distance of 39,000 meters had been made possible by enemy observation planes, high in the sky, reporting the location of hits to the ships that were firing. No matter how high the angle of fire of the guns, nor how long a range possessed by them, if there is not someone to observe the falls of the shots, the firing is of no practical use.

What about observation from the crow's nest on a ship's mast, you might ask? Seriously! Even if one were to climb to the crow's nest of the very highest mast, up to the lightning rod and battle flag, one could not see as far as 39,000 meters. Not only is the horizon at sea always shrouded in haze, but, more importantly, 39,000 meters is very much beyond the horizon.

This is because the earth is round.

"To the right twelve points. All turn!" ordered the chief of staff to the entire fleet. The Japanese main fleet, which had been running on a westerly course to escape from the enemy up to the present moment, suddenly changed its course to engage the superior enemy fleet!

The lookout in the turret mast had not yet sighted the enemy. However, in the operations center, a lieutenant commander of the naval staff plotted the positions of the enemy and the Japanese fleets on a chart and then, at intervals, announced the distance between them—"43,000 meters . . . 40,000 meters . . . 38,000 meters . . ."

The enemy fleet had also turned and was moving toward the Japanese fleet, so the distance between them was rapidly closing. The first announcement that the enemy had been sighted came from the lookout on the mast.

"34,000 meters!" barked the chief of staff.

The chief gunnery officer now issued his orders. The turtle-shaped batteries moved simultaneously, and the long-barreled guns, which emerge therefrom, were raised like necks of geese in the direction of the enemy.

"Ahhh, I see them coming," exclaimed Admiral Nagano, who had been intently searching for the enemy through his binoculars. "10, 11, 12, 13 ships! By Jove, a splendid formation," he continued.

At first sight, it seemed to be the strongest thirteen-ship fleet in the world. The grandeur presented by its ash-colored ships on the eastern horizon was so magnificent that it is no disgrace to call it the "King of the Pacific."

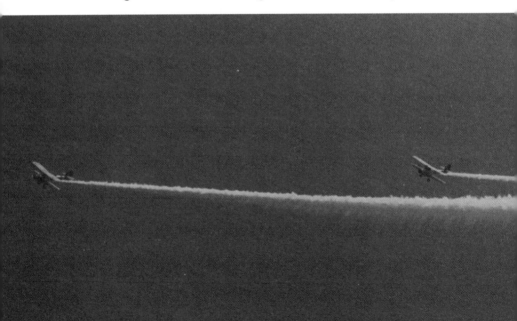

However, when the chief of staff saw the flash of guns discharging from three or four of the enemy fleet's ships, his admiration turned to pity and he snarled, "The last shot!"

The last shot? That was a funny thing for the chief of staff to say, thought the signal man. However, before two more seconds passed, he completely understood why the chief of staff had made that remark.

Just as the enemy was on the point of firing the second time, a cloud dropped like a curtain before his eyes. From above, airplanes dropped a white curtain of smoke, while from below a destroyer squadron spewed a jet-black smoke screen.

Japanese planes had now stretched a thick curtain of smoke between the two fleets, and the enemy was unable to see the Japanese ships. The distance between the fleets had been closed to 30,000 meters, which was within the range of the guns of all the enemy's capital ships. However, gunnery depended upon sight, and this fog-like smoke shut in the United States fleet like a fence of black metal.

There is a rule that when smoke, mountains, or woods obscure the view, the enemy must be struck by going over these obstacles. This is known as "indirect fire" and is one of the important principles of firing, stressed in the armies and navies of every nation in the world. Observation posts became crucial because of the need to observe where the fleet's shells were falling. Artillerymen frequently make use of mountain summits

Aircraft lay down a white smokescreen, ca. 1936. *Naval Historical Center (NH 109943)*

for observation points. As there were no mountains at sea, a plan was contrived to utilize observation planes that could observe the fall of shots from an altitude much higher than that of any mountain and then report the situation to their fleet by radio. However, the American fleet no longer had a single observation plane.

After the battle, American commander Burnett resentfully recalled this occasion. "That smoke curtain laid down by the Japanese was a great nuisance when we wanted to see their ships. We thought that we would apply indirect fire, but we did not have a single plane for observation purposes. Without a doubt, the United States fleet, with its incomparable thirteen ships—the flower of our navy, was in a dilemma."

Pity the fleet from which control of the air has been wrested by the enemy!

With the smoke curtain continuously maintained, the Japanese main fleet closed in on the enemy to a distance of 20,000 meters. The Japanese squadron commanders were exceedingly thankful at this time for their ships' 2 knots superiority in speed.

"Look, commander in chief. No matter what strategy the enemy may employ, we can control him by this extra 2 knots so that he can't get away," said the chief of staff. He continued his praise of the speed advantage, "In the long run, it has been the building policy of successive generations of naval authorities that speed is the most important thing in naval construction."

Pressing down the signal, he transmitted commands one by one to each battery:

"108 degrees—the first enemy ship."

"40-centimeter guns. By salvo!"

"Five to the left. Nineteen thousand."

At the gun batteries, the guns had been loaded several hours before, and the butts of the guns had been lowered slightly. The guns moved gently up and down with the roll of the ship.

From the round, hollowed-out observation tower behind the gun canopy dangled the battery commander's two slovenly legs. From the white shoe on the officer's right foot, a white powder kept trickling like smoke onto the head of a warrant officer below every time the officer beat a tattoo with his shoe.

"What do you see, battery commander?" inquired the warrant officer, all the while being showered with white powder from the officer's shoe.

"Well," said the officer, looking down, "I can only see a cloud of smoke." Two gunners and a pivot man sat on a narrow, cramped bench. They were manipulating the handle of an instrument that looked like the telegraph found on the bridge of a steamship and were regulating it so that the purple gauge on the outside would coincide with the moving red gauge on the inside. Suddenly, the red firing signal lamp flashed.

With quiet strength, the gun fired, and a heavy projectile, one ton in weight, left the muzzle with a loud roar, and then the great elephant-like gun snapped back into the battery. Immediately thereafter, a deafening clatter arose in the battery as the noise of the water pressure mechanism, the loading apparatus, and the battery commander's shouts combined to produce a martial cacophony. Finally, quiet was restored as a huge, polished shell was advanced by a screw device and rammed down the barrel of the gun.

"The enemy ships are completely silenced," declared the battery commander to his subordinates as he craned his neck into the battery and looked around.

Should it be said that this firing had silenced the enemy, or would it be more correct to say that the enemy had not fired a single shot in reply to ours? After all, this was not a real gun fight, for, was it not the same as ordinary target practice?

In truth, this battle was easier for the Japanese fleet than it would have been to pinch a baby's hand. Although the range was short, not a single shot came from the enemy. The Japanese planes, leisurely engaged in observation work, saw one after another of the enemy ships sink into the ocean.

"This is horrible," said the commander in chief to the chief of staff when a report was received from an observation plane that the third 40-centimeter (16-inch) gun enemy ship had foundered and sunk.

"Stop firing and advise the enemy to surrender."

Ten minutes later, the white flag was flying from the mast heads of the remaining 117 enemy ships.

That afternoon, as Admiral Nagano's combined fleet, escorting the numerous enemy prizes, moved off to the north toward Tokyo Bay, it sighted what looked like a Japanese destroyer drifting helplessly in midocean. On approaching closer, it was seen that it was the destroyer *Kurumi* with only twenty-seven survivors aboard. The commander, Lieutenant Maki, the personnel officer, and the engineering officer had all fallen in battle, and the surviving senior warrant officer was in charge of the ship. Emergency measures were taken at once to save the half-submerged hull of the ship.

The destroyer was taken in tow by one of the cruisers.

I will refrain from describing here the wild enthusiasm of the nation when Admiral Nagano's victorious combined fleet made its triumphal return to Tokyo Bay. I do this because the memory of that occasion is still too fresh in the minds of both my readers and myself.

However, I wish to add one more word. Torpedoman Kawano, who was wounded the night of the battle, received medical treatment, and was hospitalized for three months. Following this, he spent the same length of time at Beppu Hot Springs, where he received further treatment and fully recovered his health. However, although he had rendered distinguished service, he also had committed a crime, so he was sent to the naval prison at Otsu for several months to serve the remainder of his sentence for desertion. When he was released from prison and rejoined his wife, Chieko, whom he had not seen for a long time, he found out that there was now a new member of the family. A daughter with large eyes, who looked like her grandmother, had been born to him.

> Beppu
> Beppu is a city in Ōita Prefecture, on Japan's southern island Kyushu, whose hot springs have helped warriors recuperate from battle since twelfth-century samurai veterans recovered there after encounters with the Mongol army.

About six months later, Kawano and his wife, taking turns holding their baby daughter, sailed from Yokohama on *Chichibu Maru* for the new Japanese possession of Honolulu. Aboard the same ship with them rode a statue of Lieutenant Maki, which would be erected in Waikiki Park in commemoration of the Japanese victory in the war.

> *Chichibu Maru*
> *Chichibu Maru* was a luxury transpacific steamship that made a high-profile visit to Hawaii in June 1931 with Japan's Prince and Princess Takamatsu aboard. During World War II, she was renamed *Kamakura Maru* and was torpedoed by a US submarine in April 1943 while en route from Manila to Singapore. More than 2,000 Japanese soldiers and civilians perished with the ship.

Above: *Chichibu Maru* underway off Hawaii, bearing distinguished passengers from Japan, Prince and Princess Takamatsu, June 1931. *Naval Historical Center (NH 93894)*

Below: Japanese battleships *Nagato* and *Mutsu* seen from the stern of a destroyer, ca. 1936. *Naval Historical Center (NH NH 111724)*

Introduction: The First Japanese Bombshell

1. David R. Schreindl, *Sowing the Seeds of War: The* New York Times *Coverage of Japanese-American Tensions, a Prelude to Conflict in the Pacific, 1920–1941* (Provo, UT: Brigham Young University Scholars Archive, 2004), 216.

2. Hector C. Bywater, *The Great Pacific War: A History of the American-Japanese Campaign of 1931–33* (New York: Houghton Mifflin, 1925); and William H. Honan, *Visions of Infamy: The Untold Story of How Journalist Hector C. Bywater Devised the Plans That Led to Pearl Harbor* (New York: St. Martin's, 1991).

3. John J. Stephan, *Hawaii under the Rising Sun: Japan*'s *Plans for Conquest after Pearl Harbor* (Honolulu: University of Hawai'i Press, 2002), 59–61.

4. October 8, 1932, Naval Attaché/Tokyo Report: "Translations of War Articles," serial no. 150, file no. 103-400, MID 2327-H-34/1, National Archives and Records Administration (NARA) Record Group (RG) 165.

5. Ibid.

6. Ibid.

7. Ibid.

8. Ibid.

9. Richard Deacon, *Kempei Tai: The Japanese Secret Service Then and Now* (Tokyo: Charles E. Tuttle, 1990), 83.

10. December 19, 1933 letter from Office of the Assistant Chief of Staff for Military Intelligence, Headquarters Hawaiian Department, Fort Shafter, to Assistant Chief of Staff G-2, Washington, MID 2327-H-36/4, NARA RG 165.

11. "Doyle Seizes Nippon Books as Seditious," *Hawaii Hochi*, December 14, 1933; "Magazine Containing War Fiction Violates Tariff Act, Says

Doyle," *Honolulu Nippu Jiji*; "Japan Magazine with War Story Is Barred Here," clipping from unidentified newspaper; "Story of War between US and Japan Seized by Customs Men Here," *Honolulu Star Bulletin*, December 14, 1933; and "US Customs Seize Cargo of Japanese 'Fake War' Books," *Honolulu Advertiser*.

12. "Story of War between US and Japan Seized by Customs Men Here," *Honolulu Star Bulletin*, December 14, 1933.

13. December 19, 1933, letter from Office of the Assistant Chief of Staff for Military Intelligence, Fort Shafter, MID 2327-H-36/4, NARA RG 165.

14. December 15, 1933, Report No. 34953 from Lt. Col. Cortlandt Parker, US Military Attaché London, MID 2327-H-36/5, NARA RG 165.

15. "Jap Pamphlets are Confiscated," *Centralia Daily Chronicle* (Centralia, WA), December 14, 1933, 1; and "Japanese Story of War is Seized," *Dothan Eagle* (Dothan, AL), December 15, 1933, 10.

16. December 29, 1933, letter from Secretary of War George Dern to Congressman Charles J. Colden, MID 2327-H-36/2, NARA RG 165.

17. Deacon, *Kempei Tai*, 83–84.

18. Donald H. Estes, "Asama Gunkan: The Reappraisal of a War Scare." *Journal of San Diego History* 24, no. 3 (Summer 1978).

19. Jamie Bisher, *White Terror: Cossack Warlords of the Trans-Siberian* (London: Routledge, 2006), 191–96.

20. "Summaries of Communications concerning Japanese Secret Service," Exhibit VIII, p. 4, Military Intelligence, Undated (ca. 1922), National Cryptologic Museum Library, Herbert O. Yardley Collection.

21. Richard Storry, *A History of Modern Japan* (London: Penguin, 1960), 172–73.

22. Ibid.

23. John Gunther, *Inside Asia* (New York: Harper & Brothers, 1939), 58.

24. Deacon, *Kempei Tai*, 163.

25. "Japan: Blood & . . ." *Time* 15, no. 22 (June 2, 1930).

26. Herbert O. Yardley, *The American Black Chamber*, (New York: Bobbs-Merrill, 1931).

27. Gunther, *Inside Asia*, 58–59.

28. Ibid., 60.

29. Stephan, *Hawaii Under the Rising Sun*, 72–73.

30. Ian Gow, *Military Intervention in Pre-war Japanese Politics:Admiral Kato Kanji and the "Washington System"* (London: Routledge, 2012), 1–2.

31. Stephan, *Hawaii Under the Rising Sun*, 61.

32. "The Immigration Act of 1924 (the Johnson-Reed Act)," Milestones in the History of US Foreign Relations (Washington, DC: US Department of State, Office of the Historian), https://history.state.gov/milestones/1921-1936/immigration-act, accessed January 31, 2021.

33. Ibid.

34. David Kahn, *The Codebreakers: The Story of Secret Writing* (New York: Macmillan, 1973), 319–22.

35. "Japan: Blood & . . ."

36. Gow, *Military Intervention in Pre-war Japanese Politics*, 7.

37. Joseph K. Yamagiwa, ed., *Japanese Language Studies in the Showa Period: A Guide to Japanese Reference and Research Materials* (Ann Arbor: Center for Japanese Studies Publications, University of Michigan Press, 1961), https://quod.lib.umich.edu/c/cjs/ahc4455.0001.001/--japanese-language-studies-in-the-showa-period-a-guide?view=toc, accessed October 11, 2021. Fukunaga's co-author on the 1939 dictionary was Tomozane Iwakura.

38. Kyosuke Fukunaga and Katsuichi Kabashima, *Kodomo no tame no gunkan no hanashi* ("*Story of warships for children*") (Tokyo: Ichigensha, 1932); and Kyosuke Fukunaga. *Kaisho Arai Ikunosuke* (Tokyo: Morikita Shoten, 1943).

39. Gunther, *Inside Asia*, 59–60.

40. Gordon W. Prange, *Target Tokyo: The Story of the Sorge Spy Ring* (New York: McGraw-Hill, 1984), 242.

41. Joseph C. Grew, *Ten Years in Japan* (New York: Hammond, 1944), 239.

42. Foreign Relations of the United States, February 12, 1939, telegram.

43. Grew, *Ten Years in Japan*, 130.

44. "Japanese Say Suetsugu Statements 'Misquoted,'" *Japanese American* (San Francisco), January 6, 1938, 1; "Der kommende Mann Japans," *Neue Freie Presse* (Vienna), January 7, 1938; "Dreierpakt: Historische Bedingtheit," *Weltpost Hamburger Tageblatt*, February 5, 1941; "Japan vor ernsten Entschlüssen," *Hamburger Fremdenblatt*, July 4, 1941; and "Gespräch mit Suetsugo, ein Jahr Krieg im Pazifik," *Hamburger Fremdemblatt*, December 9, 1942.

45. July 31, 1946, Memorandum by General of the Army Douglas MacArthur to the Civil Affairs Division, War Department, 740.00116 PW/9-346, in *Foreign Relations of the United States*, 1946, vol. 8, *The Far East* (Washington, DC: US Government Printing Office, 1947).

46. Artsvi Bakhchinyan. "Armenian-Japanese Contacts and Literary Relations." (Yerevan: Armenian National Academy of Sciences, Institute of History, 2014), http://japanarmenia.com/armenologist-japan-2/, accessed October 12, 2021.

47. Jamie Bisher, *The Intelligence War in Latin America, 1914–1922* (Jefferson, NC: McFarland, 2016), 77.

48. Allan Beekman, *The Niihau Incident* (Honolulu, HI: Heritage Press of Pacific, 1995).

49. Harry N. Scheiber, Jane L. Scheiber, and Benjamin Jones, "Hawai'i's Kibei under Martial Law: A Hidden Chapter in the History of World War II Internments," *Western Legal History* 22, nos. 1 and 2 (2009).

50. Kim Guise, "Military Intelligence Service (MIS): Using Their Words," National WWII Museum, New Orleans, September 30, 2020, https://www.nationalww2museum.org/war/articles/military-intelligence-service-translators-interpreters, accessed February 18, 2021.

51. Douglas MacArthur, *Reports of General MacArthur*, vol. 2, part 1, *Japanese Operations in the Southwest Pacific Area* (Washington, DC: Department of the Army, 1994), 44, 58.

52. Gow, *Military Intervention in Pre-war Japanese Politics*, 2.

Fukunaga Chapter 4
1. Commander in Chief, Pacific Ocean Area, "Japanese Radio Communications and Radio Intelligence," CINCPOA Bulletin 5-45, January 1, 1945.

GLOSSARY

IJN	Imperial Japanese Navy
Jōyaku-ha	Treaty Faction
Kantai-ha	Fleet Faction
kurai tanima	"The dark valley" (era of ultra-nationalism and militarism)
MID	Military Intelligence Division (US)
NARA	National Archives and Records Administration (US)
NHC	Naval Historical Center (US)
Nichibei-sen Miraiki	Account of the Future US-Japan War
nikkei	Japanese expatriate, emigrant, or descendant (also plural)
nisei	American born offspring of Japanese immigrants (also plural)
RG	Record Group
seppuku	Ritual suicide
XO	Executive Officer
yamato damashii	Japanese fighting spirit

BIBLIOGRAPHY

Books

Beekman, Allan. *The Niihau Incident.* Honolulu, HI: Heritage Press of Pacific, 1995.

Bisher, Jamie. *The Intelligence War in Latin America, 1914–1922.* Jefferson, NC: McFarland, 2016.

Bisher, Jamie. *White Terror: Cossack Warlords of the Trans-Siberian.* London: Routledge, 2006.

Bywater, Hector C. *The Great Pacific War.* New York: Houghton Mifflin, 1925.

Deacon, Richard. *Kempei Tai: The Japanese Secret Service Then and Now.* Tokyo: Charles E. Tuttle, 1990.

Estes, Donald H. "Asama Gunkan: The Reappraisal of a War Scare." *Journal of San Diego History* 24, no. 3 (Summer 1978).

Fukunaga, Kyosuke, and Katsuichi Kabashima. *Kodomo no tame no gunkan no hanashi* ("Story of warships for children"). Tokyo: Ichigensha, 1932.

Gow, Ian. *Military Intervention in Pre-war Japanese Politics: Admiral Kato Kanji and the "Washington System."* London: Routledge, 2012.

Grew, Joseph C. *Ten Years in Japan.* New York: Hammond, 1944.

Guise, Kim. "Military Intelligence Service (MIS): Using Their Words." National WWII Museum, New Orleans, September 30, 2020. https://www.nationalww2museum.org/war/articles/military-intelligence-service-translators-interpreters, accessed February 18, 2021.

Gunther, John. *Inside Asia.* New York: Harper & Brothers, 1939.

Honan, William H. *Visions of Infamy: The Untold Story of How Journalist Hector C. Bywater Devised the Plans That Led to Pearl Harbor.* New York: St. Martin's, 1991.

Prange, Gordon W. *Target Tokyo: The Story of the Sorge Spy Ring.* New York: McGraw-Hill, 1984.

Scheiber, Harry N., Jane L. Scheiber, and Benjamin Jones. "Hawai'i's Kibei under Martial Law: A Hidden Chapter in the History of World War II Internments." *Western Legal History* 22, nos. 1 and 2 (2009).

Schreindl, David R. *Sowing the Seeds of War: The* New York Times *Coverage of Japanese-American Tensions, a Prelude to Conflict in the Pacific, 1920–1941.* Provo, UT: Brigham Young University Scholars Archive, 2004.

Scott, Len, Peter Jackson, and R. Gerald Hughes, eds. *Exploring Intelligence Archives: Documents and the History of Intelligence and International Relations.* London: Frank Cass, 2008.

Stephan, John J. *Hawaii under the Rising Sun: Japan's Plans for Conquest after Pearl Harbor.* Honolulu: University of Hawai'i Press, 2002.

Storry, Richard. *A History of Modern Japan.* London: Penguin Books, 1960.

Articles and Documents

"Customs Ban on Seditious Matter Cited." *Honolulu Star Bulletin*, December 18, 1933.

"Der kommende Mann Japans." *Neue Freie Presse* (Vienna), January 7, 1938.

"Doyle Mailing Copies to Washington." *Honolulu Star Bulletin*, December 15, 1933.

"Doyle Seizes Nippon Books as Seditious." *Hawaii Hochi*, December 14, 1933.

"Dreierpakt: Historische Bedingtheit." *Weltpost Hamburger Tageblatt*, February 5, 1941.

Foreign Relations of the United States Diplomatic Papers, 1938. Vol. 3, *The Far East.* February 12, 1939, telegram from Ambassador Grew to secretary of state, document 94 (Washington, DC: State Department Office of the Historian). https://history.state.gov/historicaldocuments/frus1938v03/d94, accessed February 13, 2021.

"Gespräch mit Suetsugo, ein Jahr Krieg im Pazifik." *Hamburger Fremdemblatt*, December 9, 1942.

"Jap Pamphlets Are Confiscated." *Centralia Daily Chronicle* (Centralia, Washington), December 14, 1933, 1.

"Japan Magazine with War Story Is Barred Here." Unidentified newspaper clipping in MID 2327, NARA RG 165. Undated [probably December 14, 1933].

"Japan vor ernsten Entschlüssen." *Hamburger Fremdenblatt*, July 4, 1941.

 Japanese War Fantasy

"Japanese Say Suetsugu Statements 'Misquoted.'" *Japanese American* (San Francisco), January 6, 1938, 1.

"Japanese Story of War Is Seized." *Dothan Eagle*, December 15, 1933, 10.

"Magazine Containing War Fiction Violates Tariff Act, Says Doyle." *Honolulu Nippu Jiji*, December 14, 1933.

Naval Attaché / Tokyo Report: "Translations of War Articles." October 8, 1932. Serial no. 150, file no. 103-400, MID 2327-H-34/1, NARA RG 165.

Office of the Assistant Chief of Staff G-2, Washington, December 19, 1933. MID 2327-H-36/4, NARA RG 165.

Reports of General MacArthur, Vol. 2, part 1, *Japanese Operations in the Southwest Pacific Area*. Washington, DC: Department of the Army, 1994, 44, 58.

Secretary of War George Dern to Congressman Charles J. Colden, December 29, 1933. MID 2327-H-36/2, NARA RG 165.

"Seized Japanese Book Reveals Propaganda for War against America." *Washington Herald*, January 15, 1934, 1.

"Story of War between US and Japan Seized by Customs Men Here." *Honolulu Star Bulletin*, December 14, 1933.

"Summaries of Communications concerning Japanese Secret Service." Undated (ca. 1922). Exhibit VIII, p. 4, Military Intelligence, National Cryptologic Museum Library, Herbert O. Yardley Collection.

"The Novel 'Nichibeisen Miraiki' (Future Japanese-American War), which Stirred a Controversy." *Nippu Jiji*, December 16, 1933.

"Tokyo Refuses to Talk about Fake War Book." *Honolulu Advertiser*, December 15, 1933.

Translation of Hinode Supplement. January 1, 1934. MID 2327-H-36/11, NARA RG 165.

"US Customs Seize Cargo of Japanese 'Fake War' Books." *Honolulu Advertiser*, December 14, 1933.

US Military Attaché London. Report No. 34953 from Lt. Col. Cortlandt Parker, December 15, 1933. MID 2327-H-36/5, NARA RG 165.

"US Studies Doyle Report on Seizure." *Honolulu Advertiser*, December 17, 1933.

"War Fiction Propaganda." *Hawaii Hochi*, December 18, 1933.

INDEX